Essential Guides for
EARLY CAREER
TEACHERS

Using Cognitive
Science in
the Classroom

Essential Guides for Early Career Teachers

The *Essential Guides for Early Career Teachers* provide accessible, carefully researched, quick-reads for early career teachers, covering the key topics you will encounter during your training year and first two years of teaching. They complement and are fully in line with the new Early Career Framework and are intended to assist ongoing professional development by bringing together current information and thinking on each area in one convenient place. The texts are edited by Emma Hollis, Executive Director of NASBTT (the National Association of School-Based Teacher Trainers), who brings a wealth of experience, expertise and knowledge to the series.

Why not explore the other books in this series?

Essential Guides for Early Career Teachers: Assessment
Alys Finch
Paperback ISBN: 978-1-912508-93-8

Essential Guides for Early Career Teachers: Mental Well-being and Self Care
Sally Price
Paperback ISBN: 978-1-912508-97-6

Essential Guides for Early Career Teachers: Special Educational Needs and Disability
Anita Devi
Paperback ISBN: 978-1-913063-29-0

Essential Guides for Early Career Teachers: Understanding and Developing Positive Behaviour in Schools
Patrick Garton
Paperback ISBN: 978-1-913453-09-1

Essential Guides for Early Career Teachers: Workload – Taking Ownership of your Teaching
Julie Greer
Paperback ISBN: 978-1-913453-41-1

Essential Guides for Early Career Teachers: Using Cognitive Science in the Classroom
Kelly Woodford-Richens
Paperback ISBN: 978-1-914171-05-5

Our titles are also available in a range of electronic formats. To order, or for details of our bulk discounts, please go to our website www.criticalpublishing.com or contact our distributor, Ingram Publisher Services (IPS UK), 10 Thornbury Road, Plymouth PL6 7PP, telephone 01752 202301 or email IPSUK.orders@ingramcontent.com.

Essential Guides for
EARLY CAREER
TEACHERS

Using Cognitive Science in the Classroom

NASBTT

Kelly Woodford-Richens
Series editor: Emma Hollis

First published in 2021 by Critical Publishing Ltd

British Library Cataloguing in Publication Data
A CIP record for this book is available from the British Library

ISBN: 978-1-914171-05-5

This book is also available in the following e-book formats:

EPUB ISBN: 978-1-914171-07-9
Adobe e-book ISBN: 978-1-914171-08-6

Cartoon illustrations by Élisabeth Eudes-Pascal represented by GCI
Cover and text design by Out of House Limited
Project management by Newgen Publishing UK
Printed and bound in Great Britain by 4edge, Essex

Critical Publishing
3 Connaught Road
St Albans
AL3 5RX

www.criticalpublishing.com

Paper from responsible sources

Contents

Meet the series editor and author   vi

Foreword   vii

1. An introduction to cognitive science   1

2. Being a human-first teacher   17

3. Great expectations   29

4. A toolkit for lesson planning   41

5. Planning and assessment: knowing your pupils and knowing what they know   57

6. Next steps: consciously incompetent to unconsciously competent   83

7. Get out there and change lives!   93

8. Conclusion   99

Acronym buster   104

Index   105

Meet the series editor

Emma Hollis

I am Executive Director of NASBTT (the National Association of School-Based Teacher Trainers) and my absolute passion is teacher education. After gaining a first-class degree in psychology I trained as a primary teacher, and soon became head of initial teacher training for a SCITT provider. I am dedicated to ensuring teachers are given access to high-quality professional development at the early stages of and throughout their careers.

Meet the author

Kelly Woodford-Richens

I was a science teacher and lead practitioner for teaching and learning in schools for more than ten years. I have recently started a role in initial teacher training, inspired and motivated by the opportunity to create a positive ripple effect by training teachers.

Foreword

As a passionate advocate of high-quality teacher education and continuing professional development, it has always been a source of frustration for me that beyond the ITT year, access to high-quality, structured ongoing professional development has always been something of a lottery for teachers. Access and support has been patchy, with some schools and local authorities offering fantastic opportunities for teachers throughout their careers, while in other locations CPD has been given lip service at best and, at worst, is non-existent.

This series was conceived of to attempt to close some of those gaps and to offer accessible professional learning to busy teachers in the early stages of their careers. It was therefore a moment of genuine pleasure when proposals for an entitlement for all early career teachers (ECTs) to receive a package of support, guidance and education landed on my desk. There is now a genuine opportunity for school communities to work together to offer the very best early career development for our most precious of resources – the teachers in our schools.

The aim of this series is to distil some of the key topics which occupy the thoughts of early career teachers into digestible, informative texts which will promote discussion, contemplation and reflection and will spark further exploration into practice. In each edition, you will find a series of practical suggestions for how you can put the 'big idea' in each chapter into practice: now, next week and in the long term. By offering opportunities to bring the learning into the classroom in a very concrete way, we hope to help embed many of the principles we share into your day-to-day teaching.

This title skilfully takes what we understand about cognitive science and applies its principles not only to your teaching but to your own professional development as a new entrant to the profession. Teaching is a complex and highly demanding job, and it is as important to understand and manage your own cognitive load as it is for you to help your pupils do the same. Kelly's insights offer practical ways for you to do this while sharpening your understanding of this important area of education research.

I hope you enjoy exploring this book as much as I have enjoyed editing it.

Emma Hollis
Executive Director, NASBTT

Chapter 1   An introduction to cognitive science

What? (The big idea)

How pupils learn and how to make learning stick

A warm welcome to this book, delivered with the strong belief that by engaging in the strategies it presents, you are going to become a brilliant teacher. So, first of all, here are some questions to consider.

>> What are cognitive science and cognitive load theory?

>> Why on earth is cognitive science important to you as an early career teacher?

>> Do you need to use it when you teach?

>> Exactly how do you use it when you teach?

Many myths exist about how you should teach; what follows is an attempt to bust those myths and explain why you should use strategies that are rooted in evidence and research. The ideas and strategies you will encounter in this book are all evidence based. Yet even with evidence-based methods of teaching the continuation of research to ensure that the teaching approaches align with the evidence is critical. A recent Education Endowment Foundation report (Education Endowment Foundation, 2021) showed more evidence is still required across year groups and subjects to further support these original works and provide even more compelling evidence. That being said, all the methods you will learn about here have been proven and undergone rigorous peer-reviewed processes to ensure they will indeed impact positively on your pupils. However, in the meantime let's return to methods that were not rooted in evidence yet we still adopted in good faith.

The first myth I encountered was when I was training to teach in 2011. We were taught to cater for pupils' learning styles to maximise assimilation of the knowledge and skills we were trying to teach. While many learning styles were proposed, they could be broadly grouped into:

» visual (learning better when you see something written down);

» auditory (learning better when you hear something);

» kinaesthetic (learning better when you do/experience something).

This was a compelling idea in principle because we could all relate to it and think, 'Yes, I prefer to learn in the kinaesthetic way' or 'I definitely learn better when I see something written down', so it made some sense to teach to learning styles. Teachers spent many hours planning lessons around VAK (visual, auditory and kinaesthetic) learning styles, a prodigious task for an early career teacher, and it was commented on during formal lesson observations. However, many studies and many years later, there is still absolutely no evidence that catering for learning styles improves pupils' outcomes; in fact, it can even have a detrimental effect on some learners (Pashler, 2009).

For long-standing experienced teachers, it can often be hard to shift their thinking or change their practice as they have seen these 'fads', such as learning styles, come and go over the years. But the beauty of cognitive load theory (CLT) is that it is rooted in rigorous, peer-reviewed research and has been proven to have a lasting positive impact on the assimilation of knowledge. See Rosenshine (2012) for a summary.

If you haven't yet come across Dylan Wiliam, you soon will (in Chapter 5 for example!). He is an expert teacher who has helped inform government education policy. In 2017, he tweeted that 'Sweller's cognitive load theory is the single most important thing for teachers to know' (Wiliam, 2017).

- In pencil, mark on the scale bar below, or in a notebook, your understanding of what cognitive load theory means and why it is important; the higher the number on the scale, the better your understanding. (Don't worry whether you're a zero or an eight; the idea is that the chapter will shift your thinking. It's always about those +1s, or even +0.1s.)

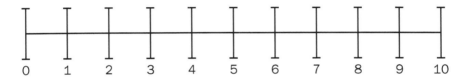

Cognitive science involves understanding how the structure and functions of the brain affect your ability to learn. It is a branch of science that considers brain architecture when thinking about how to embed learning into pupils' minds. Human cognition can be broadly divided into working memory (sometimes called short-term memory) and long-term memory. Your job as a teacher is to make sure that your pupils' learning is encoded into the brain's long-term memory so that they have confidence in and long-term retention of the knowledge and skills taught.

Working memory is activated when you receive new information, and it has limits. Do you remember Kim's Game from when you were a child? You were presented with a tray of objects, given 30 seconds to memorise them and then the tray was covered. You then had to name as many objects as you could. Some of you may even remember *The Generation Game* on the BBC, where the final task was remembering all the objects on a conveyor belt. The capacity of the working memory is roughly five to seven objects from that tray or conveyor belt; many more than that can be a struggle. Warning: here comes some theory; your working memory is about to be tested.

John Sweller (1994) notes there are three types of working memory load: intrinsic, extraneous and germane.

1. Intrinsic load refers to how complex the content is. Learning is impaired if the capacity of the working memory is overloaded when trying to penetrate the complexity. In other words, if the content is too complex, lots of space will be taken up in a pupil's working memory as they try to understand it.

2. Extraneous load refers to the instructions that pupils receive. Vague or inadequate instructions to a pupil will again overload the capacity of the working memory, meaning the pupil cannot start work. For example, if you were to give the instruction 'attempt any three questions in any order from the list of 20 but be sure to do number 5 before 6 and do not try question 12 if you have done question 7', the pupil would work so hard trying to figure out what this meant that their working memory would be overloaded before they even got to the questions!

3. Finally, germane load 'comes from the mental processes of thinking and processing information, which ultimately leads to learning'. Germane load is where you absolutely want to focus your pupils' working memory.

So, in summary: keep the content complexity accessible, give precise instructions and use teaching strategies that will activate learning (Sweller, 1994).

Now let's turn to focus on long-term memory.

Reflective task ◀◀◀

- Can you recite your favourite pop song from when you were young? (This can be surprising when you get older and haven't heard a song for 20 years but find yourself singing along.)

- How are you able to recall something you have not thought about for a long time?

Why is it that you can remember 40 lines of a song from ten years ago but if I asked what is the difference between extraneous and germane cognitive load (which you read about two minutes ago) you might struggle to answer? The answer is this: 'Memory is the residue of thought', my favourite line from Daniel T Willingham's Why Don't Pupils Like School? (Willingham, 2010). Just digest that for a moment and take in its full meaning because it underpins exactly how you are going to teach. Teaching happens in time; learning happens over time.

The reason you were able to recall the song lyrics is because at the time you practised them over and over again. You may have even thought about the song when it wasn't playing or looked up the lyrics to learn them. You certainly didn't know all of those lyrics after the first time of hearing. So, you first held the song in working memory, then parts of it went into long-term memory as you thought about it. When you re-heard the song, you thought about the lyrics more and retrieved what you already knew (probably the chorus) and added a bit each time until you could sing it fully. And now, there it sits, easily recalled forever. Which brings us to the next really important point: your long-term memory is infinite.

Therefore, if you think about things many times and activate the neurons in your brain to retrieve the information, then you can store an untold amount of information. I love this fact because it means that, while there will be some differences, it proves that everyone is capable of taking on new knowledge and learning new things, if only they practise. What a great thing to be able to stand in front of your pupils and say! And this really is true for all humans. I really recommend you read Willingham, himself a cognitive scientist; it is the first book on my beginner teachers' reading list.

Now let's look at some teaching strategies and the research evidence that shows that practices based on cognitive load theory have a positive impact on pupils' learning.

Top tip ◀◀◀

Don't worry about trying to remember all the theory here. Just store the fact that *memory is the residue of thought* and how this is going to be really important in your teaching.

Reflective task ◀◀◀

Think about a completely new skill or piece of knowledge, let's say how to Bonsai a juniper shrub.

- You are given the shrub. What do you think should happen next?

- What is the role of any expert in the room?

- Do you think all readers will approach the task in the same way and have the same feelings about it?

To get really good quality Bonsaied shrubs, I am hoping you may have come up with one or more of the following.

1. You would like to see what a good example of a completed Bonsai looks like.

2. You would like the expert in the room to show you, step by step, which branches to snip, where to add wire and what your choices are in terms of bending and shaping for good effect.

3. You would like to practise some independent shaping once you are comfortable with what you are doing.

4. You would like feedback in the moment so you can produce your best piece of work.

5. If you are struggling, you would like the expert to provide scaffolding. If you take to it, you would like the expert to push you on.

That was one example. Now let's go to an extreme: imagine you need open heart surgery. How would you feel if the surgeon just practised on you without any prior teaching, modelling, observing experts, getting feedback and then improving his or her technique under the watchful eye of the expert?

While these two examples could have very different outcomes, there was a fashion a few years back for 'discovery' or 'constructivist' learning, which somewhat mirrors this approach. Teachers were encouraged to plan these seemingly 'amazing' lessons where pupils would visit information stations with a blank proforma and collect information to fill in, say on different methods the body has for fighting disease – discovering the learning for themselves. Everyone would look busy as they moved around the room, all ending up with sheets full of facts. Had they learned anything? Did they understand the key terms? In short, no. But on the surface, it might look like they had made loads of progress.

There is extensive research showing that this approach to learning does not result in pupils assimilating knowledge; see Kirschner et al (2006) for a good example. It links back to our Bonsai and surgeon examples; the teacher is the expert in the room and should teach the knowledge, introducing new material in small steps, assessing, giving feedback and promoting thinking.

So, if you do not teach to learning styles or let pupils discover learning for themselves, what does the research evidence suggest about how you should teach? For the best paper summarising the research, see Rosenshine's 'Principles of Instruction' (Rosenshine, 2012). He, alongside Dylan Wiliam, are going to play a very formative role in how you develop as a teacher. Chapter 4 will address how you plan a lesson, but what follows is the theory sitting behind it.

Rosenshine's first principle is that you should start a lesson with a short review of previous learning. This has become known as retrieval practice, alongside interleaving and spaced practice.

- Retrieval practice is low-stakes assessment of prior learning.

- Interleaving is where you include learning from a variety of topics.

- Spaced practice is where you allow pupils 'forgetting time' before asking similar questions, say in two weeks.

Reflective task ◀◀◀

- How do you think retrieval practice, interleaving and spaced practice link to cognitive load theory?

Remember, *memory is the residue of thought*. Activating thinking about something you covered six weeks ago will lead to pupils making a plethora of noises as they try to remember. The words might sound familiar to them when you ask, for example, about the difference between a tendon and a ligament, but many will get it wrong. And that really is okay! It is low stakes because you will be really explicit in the purpose of retrieval practice: to shift learning into long-term memory by continually thinking about knowledge. This persistent asking of questions about prior learning, and revisiting ideas from previous topics until you are sure your pupils can remember them in the long term, will soon lead to growing confidence as you show them the infinite capacity of their long-term memory.

Reflective task ◀◀◀

- Think back to when you first started learning to drive. That moment when you sat in the car and the instructor started explaining the functions of the pedals, switches and levers. How did it feel in terms of cognitive overload?

- Now think about the last time you drove and let's consider that in the context of cognitive load too. Did you even think about where to put your feet and hands or what to do with the switches? Or did you automatically just arrive at your destination while singing, chatting and thinking about what to have for dinner (and maybe even eating a chocolate bar)?

Through constant thinking and practice, your brain processed and moved 'how to drive' into long-term memory. So now when you drive, your brain can host a whole range of other thinking. You have freed up all that space in your cognition just by practising. But what happens when you drive abroad for the first time? Suddenly, you can't bear to have the radio on and you certainly wouldn't be munching that Dairy Milk; your absolute focus is on all the new information your brain is receiving. However, it is likely that very soon you will get the hang of it because your vast experience of driving has given you the foundational knowledge on which to build new knowledge.

An epiphany I had while reading Willingham was this: once you have practised something enough that you can do it without thinking about it, you can add more knowledge to it. Cognitive scientists call this building schema; the more you practise recalling knowledge, ensuring it is embedded, the more you can add further knowledge, then create links between those firm banks of knowledge, which in turn allows you to add more knowledge. Willingham points out that people only like attempting tasks that are just beyond their comfort zone, because they get a buzz of adrenaline when they solve or achieve it: humans are curious but not actually good at thinking (Willingham, 2010).

This is why there may be an educational gap that gets harder to close as pupils get older. Parents who invest time in using a large vocabulary, counting when their child climbs the stairs, reading to them every night and so on, often create strong foundational knowledge for formal schooling to build on. There is likely to be a gap with children whose early formative years did not include this rich start in life. These children may find schooling extremely difficult and often feel too far out of their comfort zones – right into their panic zones. They may disengage from school, essentially because they didn't get all the practising opportunities afforded to their peers, meaning new knowledge did not have the foundation required in order to build schema. But there is hope. With your new-found understanding of long-term memory, you can just practise, practise, practise with your pupils and prove to them the infinite capacity of the mind.

Top tip ◀◀◀

Retrieval practice is going to be essential to your teaching. A really important part of it is to tell the pupils *why* they are doing it. The first time you meet them, write a long list of digits and letters on the board and challenge them to remember as many as they can. Then do the song lyric test you did above. Show them the infinite storage of long-term memory and explain that is why they are going to do retrieval practice with you.

Another fabulous teaching technique that takes account of cognitive load theory is dual coding.

Reflective task ◀◀◀

Have you ever been in a presentation where the facilitator had a fancy overcrowded PowerPoint, with either lots of images or text, or both?

* What did you do and how did you feel? Did you read the text as they spoke and so not hear what they said, or listen but not read the words?

- Were you distracted by a picture that reminded you of a person or a holiday, so you found you were not listening at all?

- Was there so much information that you felt overwhelmed and didn't really understand what the actual point was?

This is known as the redundancy effect: where your mind is directed towards redundant information that overloads the working memory and distracts from the purposeful material. And although learning styles have been discredited as a teaching strategy, there are different ways the brain receives information, for example through the visual stream or the auditory stream. This has the potential to be cognitively overloading, but if you present information slowly, step by step, both in terms of visual illustrations and teaching orally, then the working memory is not overloaded. And that is the key difference: the burdensome PowerPoint slide with non-essential information all presented in one go versus information being presented in a stepwise fashion with your attention drawn to each new piece of information, which builds on the previous one. Watch Adam Boxer in this short video for an example of this 'dual coding' www.youtube.com/watch?v=16SBht2iF_k (or search 'Adam Boxer dual coding'). You do not need to be an artist to dual code really effectively. All you need to be able to do is add small pieces of information at a time. We return to the effectiveness of dual coding and how to plan lessons incorporating it in Chapter 4.

Top tip ◀◀◀

Get yourself a mini whiteboard (MWB) and pen. All schools have them and they are going to be your absolute key piece of teaching equipment. Alternatively, invest in a graphics tablet which can save images/video for later reuse.

So what? ◀ ◀ ◀

Let's return to the questions from the start of the chapter and try and answer them.

» *What are cognitive science and cognitive load theory?* Cognitive science is understanding the architecture of the brain and how you learn; cognitive load theory is knowing that your working memory hits capacity very quickly and you have to mitigate this when you teach.

» *Why on earth is cognitive science important to you as an early career teacher?* Because learning happens over time, not in a single lesson. Remembering things long term requires practice.

» *Do you need to use it when you teach?* Absolutely, every lesson. Research shows that pupils remember more and are more confident with this approach.

» *Exactly how do you use it when you teach?* By retrieval practice (asking questions from the last lesson, last week, last term, last year), spaced practice (leaving a gap when you think pupils have 'learned' something and then testing them again), interleaving (where you include questions from different topics, not just the one you are teaching right now) and dual coding (introducing material in small visual steps while teaching the concept or idea). There will be much more on this in Chapter 4 when we get to lesson planning.

Top tip ◀ ◀ ◀

Retrieval practice can involve a low-tech, quick-fire set of questions; it can be a brain dump of 'write everything you know about...'; it can be 'write a question about each of these previous five topics for something you want to know'. My top tip is to keep it simple: write questions that you know your class have struggled with and need to go over for the best, personalised approach.

Retrieval practice

It is only worthwhile doing retrieval practice if you know which questions pupils are getting right or wrong. So much information is generated through these many quizzes that it would be impossible to take a note of every pupil's response to every single answer. Some schools may advocate the use of technology to record responses, and that is great, but there is an easy low-tech solution. Most importantly, the top tip that follows relies on you building trusting, open and honest relationships with your pupils (see Chapter 2 for the best ways to do this). But once these are established, you can follow this top tip.

Top tip ◀ ◀ ◀

As you go through each question, tell pupils it doesn't matter if they get it wrong as you will re-teach and revisit it until they can remember; then get them to raise their hands. Do this for each question and scan the room. If they all get the same question wrong, teach them the answer and put the question in again tomorrow or the next lesson. If most get it right, leave it out for a few weeks and then reintroduce it. For those that got it wrong, have a quick word once the rest of the pupils are doing an independent task. If it's an equal split, keep the question in until the majority get it right.

Metacognition

Chapter 4 focuses in depth on planning lessons, including a plethora of techniques on how to do retrieval practice and dual coding; for now, we will move onto metacognition. Cognition is about 'thinking'; going meta means 'thinking about thinking'. Without realising it maybe, reading this chapter has made you think about your thinking quite a lot. The most important thing is to teach pupils to be metacognitive because it helps them become good problem solvers and independent learners. Some basic strategies for metacognition that can support good learning when you see a challenging problem include asking: 'What did I do previously when I met a problem like this? What do I already know that can help me? What strategies do I have which I can embrace when I find something hard?' You can then at least start to tackle a problem rather than give up.

Example ◀◀◀

The questions that follow can be a really good metacognitive task, particularly if you think the content you are trying to teach is challenging. Having employed these strategies in my classroom and seen them in the classrooms of many excellent teachers, the impact is really visible and the thinking goes really deep. The scale of 1–10 can easily be changed to emojis for younger years.

1. On a scale from 1 (very unclear) to 10 (very clear), how would you rate your overall understanding of today's lesson/learning?

2. What two things did you learn today?

3. Of those two things, how confident are you that what you remember is actually correct from 1 (not confident) to 10 (very confident)?

4. What did you find difficult in the lesson?

5. What did you do when you found it difficult?

6. Would you do anything differently next time you find something difficult?

To begin with, pupils might be resistant to answering as you are making them think carefully about what they are learning, but again, this is that first bit of retrieval.

Your classes will have to sit many tests and exams, either at the end of a unit of work, the end of a year, or a key stage. This is for you to ascertain what they have remembered and can apply to new situations (hopefully if you have employed the strategies above you will be pleased!).

Before giving back the answer papers or going through the answers, it can be quite powerful to ask pupils to really reflect on how they did with a series of questions. For very early years, not all of these questions may be relevant but could be adapted. These might be something like the following list.

1. Did you prepare for the test?

2. How did you prepare (eg mind maps, note taking, writing questions)?

3. How did you think the test went?

4. What did you do when you found a question difficult?

5. Which question did you find the most difficult?

6. Which question do you think was the easiest?

7. Why do you think you found that one easy?

8. What would you do differently next time?

Getting pupils to do this immediately after they have sat the paper is really interesting and will reveal information that can be compared and discussed once their papers are returned or you go through the answers. For some of the test questions, pupils will have given up as they were too challenging. But by thinking about their approaches and responses, pupils can start to learn great insights into how they personally think. And, as you will see later, if you just give back papers with no prior reflection, the only thing pupils will focus on is their grade/mark/percentage, which will make them feel either great or terrible depending on the result of the test. In class, pupils will be honest about how much they prepared and how this relates to the final outcome; they will have opportunities to really reflect and think 'next time I will...' And when you come to the 'next time', revisit their answers and remind them of all their personal strategies that align with how they think.

Chapter 4 will revisit metacognition and how you can model it for your pupils during teaching.

Keep a bank of metacognitive questions on a PowerPoint slide or, even better, write them on the windows (more about that in later chapters!).

Summary of teaching strategies

1. Retrieval practice is the revisiting of previously taught material to repeatedly get pupils to recall knowledge, in order to embed it into long-term memory. This can be as easy as a list of questions.

2. Include questions from the last lesson, last week, last term and even last year to space out the practice and interleave your topics.

3. Explain to the pupils why you do these low-stakes quizzes and do a hands-up assessment to see what they are transferring to long-term memory.

4. Use dual coding, where appropriate, to allow two streams of the same information to go into the brain as this will aid learning.

5. Employ metacognitive strategies to make pupils think about their thinking, making them self-aware and thus equipping them to become more confident and to rely on past experiences to help them.

Now what? ◀◀◀

Practical task for tomorrow ◀◀◀

This chapter has given a whistle-stop tour of cognitive science and how it impacts learning. Look at a lesson you are teaching and dedicate the first ten minutes to retrieval practice. Remember, this is not just a recap of the last lesson only. Plan some questions that include knowledge that you are not sure your pupils are secure in. Think about what you will do when they raise their hands to tell you how they did.

Practical task for next week ◀◀◀

When you come to a lesson that has particularly challenging content, or if you are doing an assessment of any kind, plan some of the metacognitive questions above. Again, think about what you will do with the information this generates. Plan your conversations with the pupils about their thinking and how thinking about their thinking improves learning.

Practical task for the long term ◀◀◀

Keep cognitive load at the heart of every lesson you teach. Think about the new knowledge your pupils are assimilating and how you are dependent on the acquisition of previous knowledge for new learning to be taken on. Make sure retrieval practice becomes normal routine, and never stop telling the pupils why they are doing it.

Reflective task ◀◀◀

- Do you have a new-found or deeper understanding of cognitive load theory and how this impacts how you are going to teach? Mark your scale bar again. Hopefully it is further on than at the start of the chapter.

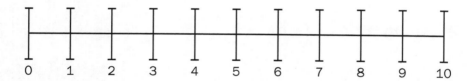

What next? ◀◀◀

This chapter has provided the theory to underpin your practice. You have learned that pupils cannot discover new learning for themselves but will rely on you, as the expert in the room, to guide them to become independent thinkers. Chapter 4 delves into how to plan lessons, taking what cognitive science teaches us into account, but first we will purposefully deviate and think about what it will be like for you as you take those first steps into being a professional teacher. Chapter 2 explores how you are going to build trusting relationships with your pupils which allow you to get to the exciting bit of imparting your passion for your subject or topics!

Further reading

Curated research and resources: Klaskit (2020) A Collection of Retrieval Practice Research and Resources. [online] Available at: https://klaskit.com/a-collection-of-retrieval-practice-research-and-resources (accessed 6 September 2021).

Free Seneca courses on cognitive science: Seneca (2019) Free Cognitive Science CPD Course for Teachers. [online] Available at: https://senecalearning.com/en-GB/blog/free-cognitive-science-level-2-cpd-course (accessed 6 September 2021).

Cognitive Science 1: Seneca (2021) Cognitive Science for Teachers. [online] Available at: https://app.senecalearning.com/classroom/course/9f6bf15c-23fe-401c-810a-3bc66d761885 (accessed 6 September 2021).

Cognitive Science 2: Seneca (2021) Cognitive Science for Teachers Level 2. [online] Available at: https://app.senecalearning.com/classroom/course/aebdbb79-c863-4eca-ab3f-31e5120f5fb0 (accessed 6 September 2021).

Metacognition for teachers: Seneca (2021) Metacognition for Teachers. [online] Available at: https://app.senecalearning.com/classroom/course/d1277cd6-7205-4511-8d95-1f1ed341ae69 (accessed 6 September 2021).

The Learning Scientists: The Learning Scientists [online] Available at: www.learningscientists.org (accessed 6 September 2021).

Tom Sherrington blog: Teacherhead (2019) 10 Techniques for Retrieval Practice. [online] Available at: https://teacherhead.com/2019/03/03/10-techniques-for-retrieval-practice (accessed 6 September 2021).

Unleash the science of learning: Retrieval Practice [online] Available at: www.retrievalpractice.org (accessed 6 September 2021).

References

Education Endowment Foundation (2021) *Cognitive Science Approaches in the Classroom.* [online] Available at: https://educationendowmentfoundation.org.uk/public/files/Publications/Cognitive_science_approaches_in_the_classroom_-_A_review_of_the_evidence.pdf (accessed 7 September 2021).

Kirschner, P A, Sweller, J and Clark, R E (2006) Why Minimal Guidance During Instruction Does Not Work: An Analysis of the Failure of Constructivist, Discovery, Problem-Based, Experiential, and Inquiry-Based Teaching. *Educational Psychologist*, 41(2): 75–86.

Pashler, H (2009) Learning Styles: Concepts and Evidence. *Psychological Science in the Public Interest*, 9(3): 105–19.

Rosenshine, B (2012) Principles of Instruction: Research-Based Strategies That All Teachers Should Know. *American Educator*, Spring: 12–39.

Sweller, J (1994) Cognitive Load Theory, Learning Difficulty, and Instructional Design. *Learning and Instruction*, 4(4): 295–312.

Wiliam, D (2017) I've come to the conclusion Sweller's Cognitive Load Theory is the single most important thing for teachers to know. Twitter, 26 January. [online] Available at: https://twitter.com/dylanwiliam/status/824682504602943489 (accessed 7 September 2021).

Willingham, D T (2010) *Why Don't Pupils Like School? A Cognitive Scientist Answers Questions About the Mind* (1st ed). San Francisco: Jossey-Bass.

Chapter 2　Being a human-first teacher

What? (The big idea)

What does it mean to be a human-first teacher?

Well, this is very exciting: you're going to be a teacher. You have just had an introduction to the overarching and rigorous principles of cognitive science. Historically, books on cognitive science and teaching manuals have been written to support understanding of how the pupils you teach learn. Principally, these books provide the theory and sometimes strategies you can use to help support reliable transference of information from pupils' working memories to their long-term memories. You have, in the previous chapter and maybe for the first time, heard phrases such as 'dual coding', 'retrieval practice' and 'cognitive load theory', among many others. An experienced teacher may be able to simply layer these techniques into an already-established practice without overload until they become part of their vernacular. However, the difference with this book is that it also applies those very same cognitive principles to you. As a novice teacher, you need to take in an immense amount of information. You have to learn techniques, acquire the teaching craft and be a fully-fledged independent teacher in a relatively short space of time. For the first time, this book recognises the impact of cognitive load theory on early career teachers such as yourself.

To this end, there will be retrieval and spaced practice as you go through, making you, the reader, reflect back on learning from previous chapters. The more you think about previous ideas, the more you are firing those connections and transferring this new information into your own long-term memory. This will allow your confidence to grow as you realise just how much you can remember.

Furthermore, this serves as a model for how you will teach your own pupils. By being fully immersed in the techniques of cognitive science, you will recognise their value and be persuaded that strategies such as retrieval and spaced practice, as well as metacognitive approaches to learning, truly work. So, do not be alarmed if the reflective tasks sometimes seem to bear little resemblance to the chapter title: this is intentional. These tasks are functional to reinforce the idea that you only remember what you think about: *'memory is the residue of thought'* (Willingham, 2010).

But before you get to decode the craft of teaching and empower yourself to create and deliver excellent lessons (as set out in later chapters and founded in cognitive science), we need to lay some robust foundations of principles that are important before you even step into a classroom. This is the other thing that sets this book apart from other 'how to teach' scripts; it will make you think deeply about your drive and your passion and how you can harness this to full effect in the classroom. To be a great teacher (and that does not necessarily just mean planning and delivering a high-brow lesson on molar calculations), it is important to examine how critical it is to be a *human-first teacher.* This is the big idea of this chapter. You're going to need a natty notebook for the following bit (another great thing about teaching is the joy of new stationery). Let's go straight into some tasks.

Reflective task ◀◀◀

- In pencil, mark on the scale bar your understanding of what 'human-first teaching' might mean to you and why it is important; the higher the number on the scale, the better your understanding. (Don't worry whether you're a zero or an eight; the idea is that the chapter will shift your thinking.)

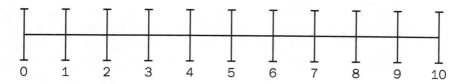

Reflective task ◀◀◀

- Think back to school and your own favourite teachers. List on paper or in your notebook three things they did that transformed you in some way.

- Then think of a teacher whose classroom was not a place you enjoyed. Write three things that meant you did not relish that subject or environment so much.

- Now examine your list and reflect deeply on it. Maybe ask your friends and family the same questions. While a good proportion of your answers may indeed relate to a particular passion for a subject, most of the impact a teacher has relates to how they made their pupils *feel*. Is that true for you? Did you engage more in the lessons where you knew the teacher cared? This reflection is metacognitive: you are thinking about your thinking. This big idea is important because if you too become a human-first teacher you have laid the foundations on which to build a great educator.

Top tip ◀◀◀

'They don't care what you know until they know that you care.'

(originally Theodore Roosevelt)

Digest the above quotation and see how it relates to what you wrote about your own teachers. Did you enjoy the lessons more when you felt your teacher cared about you? What does it mean to you and the teacher you want to be? The top tip is to remember this phrase *every* time you walk into a class to teach.

Reflective task ◀◀◀

- Watch Jaz Ampaw-Far give her 'Everyday Heroes' TEDx talk and Rita Pierson's 'Every Kid Needs a Champion' videos on YouTube (see the links at the end of the chapter). How did they make you feel?

So what? ◀◀◀

Teachers have an impact that reaches far beyond a passion for their subject. People talk about them at dinner parties and with their friends and families for the rest of their lives: teachers leave an indelible mark that can't be erased. So, let's go all Simon Sinek and start with 'why?' (Sinek, 2011). This is a really important step before you get to the 'how' and 'what' of teaching and before you utilise cognitive science to help deliver excellent lessons.

Reflective task ◀◀◀

- Write down three reasons *why* you applied to train to teach. Be really authentic and examine how these resonate with you as a person. How do they manifest in other aspects of your life? Do the 'essences' of you as a person spill over into why you want to work in education?

It is likely that your reasons to train to teach aren't going include the luxurious, jet-setting lifestyle the pay would afford you. But I do expect your list features in some guise 'to make a difference'. And indeed, you are going to do this every single day: teaching is the best and most important job in the world. Let's look at a few reasons why; case-study this idea and see how they align with your own 'why'.

Real life stories

Think back to Jaz's video. I have met her many times and she is an incredible human. She has inspired me in so many ways and was in fact the one who taught me the phrase 'human-first teaching'. She has told me how every day she was steadfast in her determination to get detentions so she could stay in her 'safe place' at school and how, despite her rudeness, one teacher would ask how she was every single day. One individual teacher listened to her crazy ideas and inspired her to want to be a teacher herself. Jaz is one of millions of children throughout history whose trajectory has been changed because of teachers. Because they cared about her as a person and believed in her.

Many pupils you teach will have indescribable home lives. Here is a tough reality you will face: the incidence of neglect, abuse in many forms, drug misuse and general poor welfare is far higher than you can imagine, which is tragic. For many children it is likely that school is the only place where adults model appropriate behaviour. It is a safe space where they can witness people being polite, kind and respectful. Most importantly, it is a place where they can feel valued. I hope to convince you that it is your moral duty to help change the trajectory of these children. How does this fit with your 'why' and your reasons to train to teach? Again, this metacognitive task is making you think about your thinking. By thinking about your 'why' and how it might be important, your thinking is going a lot deeper. Furthermore, by establishing this link between your 'why', assuming it is to make a positive difference, and the huge impact you are going to have as a teacher, you are strengthening the passion, drive and determination to do a job brilliantly and change someone's life.

Next explore your passion for a subject or subjects and how this might impact the young people you are in front of. Secondary teachers generally teach one subject whereas primary teachers teach all subjects, but your absolute passion is likely to be a subset of subjects or topics.

Reflective task ◀◀◀

- Reflect on how igniting this passion in a pupil might affect you and how it aligns with your 'why'. How might it feel that you have inspired someone to pursue a career in art, maths or geography? How many other jobs in the world have that deep personal impact?

At the start of taking on a new GCSE group, I ask the class how many intend to take a science A level. It is inexpressible how it makes you feel at the end of Year 11 when, faced with the same question, a sea of hands thrusts up: this is how you can change the course of a young life. Now is that because I have a passion for my subject? Yes, in part. But more importantly, those pupils bought into me as a teacher because they knew I cared about them as individuals and I made them believe they 'could'. At primary school in Year 5, my daughter did a topic on the Holocaust. The teacher taught her with such zest and brilliance that my daughter became near obsessed: she has just completed her history degree at UCL. That is the impact you are going to have, many times over. And so it comes full circle: one or more of your teachers helped determine your path, and now you are going to do that for others.

Top tip ◀◀◀

When meeting a class for the first time, give them all a sticky note. Ask pupils to write down 'I wish my teacher knew that...' If teaching early years, some support may be required. Suggestions to get them started could include: 'I am very shy and find it really hard to answer questions out loud in front of the class', or 'I am quite disorganised and find it hard to complete homework', or 'I need to check I know what to do before I start a task', or 'I struggle with maths', or anything completely open! When you read these I promise you that you will be blown away by the responses. Not only can you support your pupils better; they now have more evidence that you care about them. Even better will be when you refer back to the sticky notes at the end of the year and see how your support has helped that shy pupil gain confidence, or you have changed their mind about a subject.

Time for a quick revisit of previously learned material from Chapter 1. Importantly, if you do not know the answer, sit and think about it. Try and visualise what you read and the concrete examples given. Even more importantly, if you cannot remember, that's okay. Be kind to yourself; just check back. Learning takes place over time, not in the moment, even if you understood it when you read it.

- What is retrieval practice? (Check back to page 6 for the answer.)

- What is dual coding? (Check back to page 8 for the answer.)

- What is metacognition? (Check back to page 11 for the answer.)

Short interlude over; now back to how you can be that human-first teacher. You are likely to have a class or tutor group for whom you have overall responsibility for their pastoral care. As a primary teacher, you will have the same class every single day for the whole year and develop a deep awareness of them as young people. As a secondary teacher, it is quite possible to start with a Year 7 tutor group and then oversee their pastoral care until they leave in Year 11. Both groups of children will have a whole host of complicated issues from friendship issues to social media bullying to dealing with puberty. You are going to be a constant source of reassurance, kindness, mediation, trust and, dare I say it, fun. The relationship with a tutor group is very different from that of a subject teacher, but is just as important, and probably mirrors the relationship between the primary teacher and their class. It is extremely rewarding to watch them blossom from shy to confident, or to notice how your mentoring helps turn around the behaviour of a challenging child and lets them engage in their learning. So, an aspect of being a teacher that you may or may not have considered is this wider role. You will be their 'go to' when things aren't going well, the point of home contact, the person they confide in. How does this fit with your 'why'? How does it make you feel that you will shape the formative years of young people?

Top tip ◀◀◀

On one of your windows near the door, use chalk pens to write the following as a list: Feeling great!; Am good thanks; I'm fine; I'm a bit worried; I'm having a tough time. If teaching very early years you could use pictograms instead. Get your class or tutor group to write their names on sticky notes that can freely move between the headings. Establish a culture of pupils moving them and being open about how they feel. This will show that you care about them by talking about their sticky note placements and will be a powerful tool. Some can become whole-class celebrations: 'Tell us why you're feeling great, Matt', or some can be a quiet word: 'Evie, I noticed you put your sticky note on "I'm worried", what can I do to help?'

Some pupils think they 'can't do it'. 'It' being PE, English, science or any subject. This is often horribly reinforced at home, where parents hold on to the strong belief that they are poor at a subject, which explains why their child is too. This is the biggest misconception of teaching and takes a lot of work to undo. But you can! The actual 'how' of structuring lessons using cognitive science as a framework is investigated in detail in later chapters, but it has to be couched in persuasive language that tells your pupils that *you believe they can do it*. This deep learning does take time, but you will find that when you continually tell your pupils they will be able to 'get it' and how much you believe in them, and then see the results, the impact is indescribable.

Reflective task ◀◀◀

- How would it feel to have a pupil or group of pupils for whom you are responsible growing in confidence? Does this dovetail with your 'why'? Are you penetrating the 'big idea' of being a human-first teacher?

Case studies

Teaching and learning

There was a class I knew of several years ago. This class was full of pupils who knew they were 'bottom set' and held deep beliefs about their poor ability, which impacted hugely on their self-esteem and in turn their behaviour. By telling them we (note the 'we') were all going to pass and not faltering from that message, the teacher went on a journey with the class, and they all passed their GCSE. The use of cognitive science informed teaching supported by unwavering language around this belief allowed the class to believe they 'could do' science.

Another example is a pupil I knew of who had special educational needs and disabilities (SEND). In particular, they had poor processing skills, which impacted on their self-belief that they could understand and remember things. Again, the methods of teaching were all founded in cognitive science, backed up with positive language. Despite not being taught by the same teacher in later years, every time they saw the teacher in the corridor, they would shout things like: 'I can still do science; I remember everything!' It made all the hard work of teaching just so worth it for that teacher.

Pastoral

Finally, I remember a child in a tutor group. They came from a separated family and had an abusive step-father. This child's self-esteem was so battered that they misbehaved constantly, did not engage with learning and were constantly in detention in Years 7 and 8. For five years they were told they were valued, they were believed in, they were liked and that they could make things different for themself. They were equipped with pens every day, coached and taught how to revise in the teacher's break times. Years 10 and 11 saw a different child who ended up passing every single GCSE. Now, one teacher cannot and would not take whole responsibility for turning that child around, but I believe that their kindness helped heal some fractures in the child's sense of self that facilitated their engagement with school life.

These case studies are but a few anecdotes. But they are representative of what all human-first teachers will experience, I promise. My most recent card says: 'Miss, I can't thank you enough for understanding me and the way I learn. No teacher has ever had as big of an impact on me as you have had. I can't put into words the exact effects you have had on me but beyond positive'. He was a very disengaged Year 11, and I will always remember those words. This will be you one day too, tears in your eyes as you realise the difference you have made.

Top tip ◀◀◀

Use those chalk pens again to write on your windows: 'I believe in you'; 'I value you'; 'I love teaching you'. And any other statements that show your pupils that you are more than just their teacher.

Let's revisit our big idea: To be the best educator, you need to be human-first in your approach and that means knowing about, caring for, believing in, trusting and facilitating young people to be the best versions of themselves. Only then can you get to the teaching of the required skills and knowledge.

Top tip ◀◀◀

Tell your pupils how much you care about them, how passionate you are about teaching or your subject, how you are on a journey with them and believe in every one of them. And do this a lot, not as a one-off at the beginning of term.

- Another bit of retrieval: you have thought about the impact your own teachers had on you. You have thought about how it might feel if a pupil was inspired by your passion for your subject. You have examined in detail your own 'why' you are training to teach. You have thought about the home lives of some pupils and how you are responsible for their pastoral care as well as delivering a curriculum. You are going to make a difference and being human-first will make pupils buy into you, and then by default into what you are trying to teach them. Once you have reflected on all of this, you should be feeling like a hero right now.

Top tip ◀◀◀

Use the **GROW** coaching model to structure conversations when supporting young people in your care. Help them to be metacognitive and empower them to take control of whatever the situation is that they are struggling with. **G**: what is your absolute **g**oal with this situation? How would it feel to reach that goal? **R**: what is your **r**eality now; how far are you from that goal? **O**: what **o**ptions do you have in order to take decisive steps; some will work, some won't. **W**: what **w**ill you do now? Write it down and commit to making either small or big changes in order to reach that goal.

Now what? ◀ ◀ ◀

Practical ways to implement this in your classroom: tomorrow, next week, next year

Practical task for tomorrow ◀◀◀

- We have explored human-first teaching and some practical ways to implement it in your classroom. Answer the following questions and have a self-conversation about your next steps and so that you are ready to GROW.

  - **G** – Is your *goal* to be a human-first teacher? Would you like to be that teacher that makes a difference?

  - **R** – In *reality*, how has the chapter provided you with an idea of what it means to be a human-first teacher and how is it aligned to your 'why'?

- **O** – What are your *options*? Look back at the top tips and your notes to help you reflect on practical strategies that will support you to be a human-first teacher. Which ones could you do?

- **W** – Commit. Which ones *will* you do? Can you think of any others? Write down a statement that says: 'In my classroom I will ... to ensure I am a human-first educator'.

- Look at your 'I will' list and choose one or more you can implement quickly, whether it is with your class(es), your tutor group or a group of pupils for whom you are responsible. Plan it now: if it is something you are going to say to them, write down the pertinent message you want to convey; or if it is a more practical strategy, do you have the resources you need (eg sticky notes or chalk pens)?

Practical task for next week ◀◀◀

Schedule this next activity in your diary to ensure you remember to do it, again being cognisant of your working memory and how much it is taking in! Stand in your classroom and just look around with fresh eyes. Does the room have the character and feeling you want to convey to show the pupils how much they are valued? What else could you add from your 'I will' list? Could you use one of the chalk pens/sticky note activities? Have you been inspired to come up with your own strategy? (I would love to hear about it!) If you are at the training stage of your career, I am sure your mentor would support you in implementing a strategy.

Practical task for the long term ◀◀◀

As stated right at the beginning of the chapter, it is likely you came into teaching to 'make a difference'. This chapter has examined how this relates to your personal 'why', and the next chapters will focus on the 'how' of teaching. However, it is pertinent to say that teaching is a demanding profession. You need to keep central to your ethos and remember what a difference you are making by being a human-first teacher. This is what makes the profession so rewarding. So, the next task is for you to 'scrapbook' the evidence that demonstrates the impact you are making. Every email you get from a parent, print it. Every card you get from a pupil or parent, keep it. Every time a pupil says something that makes your heart sing, write it on a sticky note. By storing all of these in a scrapbook or folder, you can reflect at the end of every term or year on how all the work you have done to be a human-first teacher has translated into something quite wonderful.

- Do you have a new-found or deeper understanding of what a human-first teacher is? Do you feel more confident about the importance of it? Mark your scale bar again, and hopefully it is further on than at the start of the chapter.

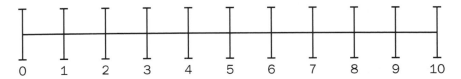

What next? ◀ ◀ ◀

You should now know the importance of showing young people that you care not just about their learning, but about them as individuals. Next time you are teaching or observing, you will be able to put this into practice. The benefits will become apparent over time. Use your list of 'I will...' to ensure you implement the practical strategies suggested or ones of your own. At the end of the chapter are some suggested links to further show the superpower of a teacher. To finish off I would like to share a quote. Haim G Ginott wrote:

> *I've come to the frightening conclusion that I am the decisive element in the classroom. It's my personal approach that creates the climate. It's my daily mood that makes the weather. As a teacher, I possess a tremendous power to make a child's life miserable or joyous. I can be a tool of torture or an instrument of inspiration. I can humiliate or heal. In all situations, it is my response that decides whether a crisis will be escalated or de-escalated and a child humanized or dehumanized.*

(Ginott, 1972)

You should now be fired up ready to get really stuck into the practicalities of using research-informed methodology to plan lessons. It's going to be great fun!

Further reading

Every kid needs a champion: Pierson, R (2013) Every Kid Needs a Champion. TED Talk. [online] Available at: www.youtube.com/watch?v=SFnMTHhKdkw (accessed 6 September 2021).

The power of a teacher: Saenz, A (2015) The Power of a Teacher. TEDx Talks. [online] Available at: www.youtube.com/watch?v=AyogyD7vXbw (accessed 6 September 2021).

The power of everyday heroes: Ampaw-Farr, J (2017) The Power of Everyday Heroes. [online] Available at: www.youtube.com/watch?v=q3xoZXSW5yc (accessed 6 September 2021).

What makes a good teacher great? Terronez, A (2017) What Makes a Good Teacher Great? [online] Available at: www.youtube.com/watch?v=vrU6YJIe6Q4 (accessed 6 September 2021).

Ampaw-Farr, J (2021) *Because of You, This is Me* (forthcoming).

When the chips are down with Rick Lavoie: Lavoie, R (1996) When the Chips Are Down. [online] Available at: www.youtube.com/watch?v=Yd4JfAH_CGI (accessed 6 September 2021).

References

Ginott, H (1972) *Teacher and Child: A Book for Parents and Teachers*. New York: The Macmillan Company.

Sinek, S (2011) *Start with Why: How Great Leaders Inspire Everyone to Take Action*. London: Penguin.

Willingham, D (2010) *Why Don't Pupils Like School? A Cognitive Scientist Answers Questions About the Mind* (1st ed). San Francisco: Jossey-Bass.

Chapter 3   Great expectations

What? (The big idea)

How will having high expectations empower you to be a great teacher?

First of all, here are some questions to ponder.

» What does 'expectations' even mean?

» How do you create a culture of high expectations?

» How does being a human-first teacher help?

» How does this link to cognitive science?

» And how can all of this empower you?

This chapter addresses these questions.

I remember standing in front of a class to deliver my first starter. My brain was full of fear: about the environment and the pupils looking at me, pulsating worry about how the pupils might behave and what the class teacher would think of me. I was hugely cognitively overloaded and could barely even think about the lesson content.

Most trainees, when asked at interview 'what do you think your biggest challenge will be?' will respond with 'managing behaviour'. The responsibility is huge; how can you deliver your lesson when a large part of your cognition is taken up with worry about the children and their behaviour? What you need to do here is reduce the 'redundancy effect', ie filter all the unhelpful environmental stimuli out and allow yourself to draw from your long-term memory and teach your lesson. It is vital to address this during your early training, equipping yourself with a go-to toolkit so your brain can focus on the knowledge acquisition of your pupils. As you progress from an early career teacher to an expert teacher, this extraneous load of worry is reduced because you become unconsciously competent. So, the aim of this chapter is to give you the confidence to teach your lessons without being cognitively overloaded by anxiety. The previous chapter gave you a deeper understanding of the importance of being a human-first teacher, and trust me when I say that this is going to be half the battle. When pupils know you care about them, they generally find it much harder not to meet your expectations. Let's start with some reflections; you will need your notebook again.

Reflective task ◀◀◀

- In pencil, mark on the scale bar your understanding of what 'high expectations' might mean to you and why it is important. The higher the number on the scale, the better you feel your understanding to be. (Again, don't worry whether you're a zero or an eight; the idea is that the chapter will shift your thinking. It's always about those +1s, or even +0.1s.)

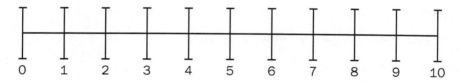

```
0   1   2   3   4   5   6   7   8   9   10
```

Essentially, setting high expectations means establishing a set of 'rules' for your classroom and letting pupils know what will happen if they fail to meet those expectations.

Reflective task ◀◀◀

- Reflect on what expectations, or rules, you think you need to establish the first time you meet a class. Write at least one non-negotiable.

There are two important points here: the first is that you cannot 'expect' a behaviour from pupils; you must teach pupils how to behave. Tom Bennett is an expert in the field of behaviour and I urge you to watch his webinars or read his books, *The Behaviour Guru* and *Running the Room* (Bennett, 2010, 2020). He strongly advocates that the teaching of behaviour is a curriculum in itself. Just reflect on that for a moment. Linked to this, Paul Dix argues that when the adults change, everything changes – another powerful endorsement of human-first teaching (Dix, 2017). I absolutely agree that teaching behaviour should be a prerequisite to any learning of the curriculum. Remember those pupils from the previous chapter who need you to model polite and respectful relationships? The chapter stressed the importance of creating and culturing a classroom where pupils feel valued because school may be the one safe place in their lives. However, it is much deeper than that. The second point is this: for some children, you can't expect them to be able to self-regulate and know that it is wrong to call out, or be physical with other children, or swear, because these are their experiences of 'normal'. So that is why behaviour should be a curriculum in itself and weave its way into your teaching lexicon. Teaching behaviour and getting it right in your classroom is often called Behaviour for Learning (BfL).

Reflective task ◀◀◀

- Once again, we are going to look back briefly at previous chapters. By thinking and reflecting on them, you will fire those neurons and help embed your learning into your long-term memory. As before, it does not matter if you need to flick back to check, but do try and think hard first.

  - What is retrieval practice? Give two ways you could conduct this with your class. (Check back if you need a reminder.)

  - Why does dual coding help pupils remember better? (Check back if you need a reminder.)

  - What three strategies, either from the previous chapter or those of your own, are you going to use to establish human-first teaching in your classroom?

- Did you notice the first two questions were slightly increased in difficulty from the first time you were asked to retrieve this information? For example, in the last chapter you were simply asked 'what is retrieval practice?' but this time you were asked to give two methodologies. This layering will deepen thinking and help transfer the useful information. How do you find thinking about your previous learning: is it difficult? Can you start to see the benefits of revisiting reading?

Back to the task in hand and how to manage behaviour in your classroom. The last question of this retrieval practice section was deliberate, because you have laid the foundations for how you are going to establish routines for the behaviour that you will expect. You have told the pupils they are valued, important, that you care about them. Adding to this 'script' (and it should be a script you repeat most lessons) is that part of caring about them is that you get to teach them about the wonders of the subject or the topic they are studying. The very first time you meet the class, you are going to tell them your expectations; behaviour management is hard to do retrospectively. Keep it simple; that way, everyone can remember.

Top tip ◀◀◀

Once you have introduced yourself and said the above, tell the class you have one rule: *The one-voice rule.* This means that when one person is speaking, everyone else is to listen; this rule applies whether it is an adult in the room or a child answering a question.

You will have to model this, teach this and explain why it is important in terms of respecting each other. But largely, communicate that as humans we do not possess the ability to effectively listen and talk at the same time; therefore, if they are talking while you are teaching then they will not be learning.

And this is the bit to get right as soon as you start talking to a class: the microsecond another person starts to talk, pause, even if mid-word; look at them and smile. Once they stop talking, say 'thank you' and continue. Here you will use lots of non-verbal communication as a reminder of your 'one-voice' rule. Do not deviate from this. Sometimes you may stand for a minute (which could feel like an eternity) looking at someone to intimate they need to wrap up their chat. You do not need to shout; just stand and use your non-verbal communication. Still keeping it simple but thinking about when the class is in flow, or coming to the time to end a task, you will need a way to draw attention to your one-voice rule. In secondary, a very simple, fairly slow '3, 2 and 1' will bring focus to you. To achieve the same aim in primary, an effective technique can be a call and response clap pattern started by the teacher and completed by the children. Sometimes a little volume, but not shouting, is needed on the '3' or the first clap, but as you establish your routine, the children will respond.

Reflective task ◀◀◀

- Does the one-voice rule align with the expectations and non-negotiable you had above? If you were in a meeting and started chatting to the person next to you, and the facilitator stopped talking to attend to your off-task chat, how would you feel? Would it change your behaviour or would you carry on talking?

There are three possible outcomes when you attempt to enforce your one-voice rule.

1. The pupil quickly stops talking; you thank them, smile and carry on with your teaching.

2. The pupil takes a while to notice you; other pupils do, the talking pupil finally notices and you thank them, smile and carry on with your teaching.

3. Now here's the thing; because you are coming from a human-first teaching place, I can honestly say this last one is the rarest. It is when a pupil realises you are waiting and makes the choice to carry on with their conversation. You may now address them by name and start to follow your school's behaviour policy.

School behaviour policies will vary from school to school but essentially include steps to take if a pupil fails to meet your expectations. These usually entail something like:

1. a warning/reminder about how to behave correctly and why it is important;

2. if the behaviour continues, move the pupil to another seat in the room;

3. if the behaviour continues, instruct the pupil to stand outside or go to a senior member of staff's classroom (often meaning automatic after-school detention in secondary school).

This segues neatly into the next top tip.

Top tip ◀◀◀

Be consistent. Pupils will feel safe if they know that you are kind but fair and just, following the school rules yourself. Using your school's behaviour policy is the easiest way to be consistent. Print it out, carry it around, write it on the board or use chalk pens to write the main points on a window to refer to. But another top tip: keep reminding pupils that you do not actually want to send them out; you really want them to stay so you can teach them.

Ultimately, all behaviour is communication. Think about a crying baby and a fraught parent at three o'clock in the morning and how difficult it can be to cope with this. But babies are just communicating a need: hunger; sore tummy; tired (there's the irony) etc. They are not trying to upset you. When a pupil is not behaving the way you would like, for example by shouting, even swearing, refusing to work or other unacceptable behaviour, it is not that they have woken up and thought: 'I know,

I will upset Miss today'. They are communicating that their needs are not being met in some way; so, we come full circle back to being that human-first teacher who tells them you like them, you care, you understand something is making them unhappy but if their behaviour continues, they will not be able to stay in the room. It is quite likely that you might just reach them. But if pupils cannot meet your expectations of behaviour, you must absolutely remember it is not personal and they are merely communicating. Do not let the fact you have worked so hard to be kind, but it wasn't received, affect you; sometimes external factors are so huge in a pupil's life that you just can't help them in that moment. What is important, alongside not taking it personally, is to be resilient and consistent and try again next lesson.

Reflective task ◀◀◀

- In your notebook, draw a circle titled '16 year-old me' if you teach secondary or '11 year-old me' if you teach primary. Now think back to being that age and draw a spider diagram of all that was really important to you. What influenced you? What made you happy?

I am happy to guess friends is quite high up here! Maybe music, family, going out, reading books etc. And while the previous chapter really stressed the impact that teachers had on you and that you will definitely have on your pupils, sometimes it is often as they leave school or even later in life that this really crystallises, which is unfortunate. The point I am trying to make is this: children don't necessarily rate teachers as 'cool' so that is why you have to work hard to make them want to be in your 'circle of trust'. If you are a human-first teacher who makes pupils feel valued, they will want to buy in to you and your expectations because it will make them feel good. Being inside the circle feels better.

Top tip ◀◀◀

Praise in public; admonish in private. If a pupil behaves well or produces a great answer or piece or work, celebrate this with the whole class. However, if a pupil is not following your expectations, set the whole class a quick question to think about, approach the pupil in question and crouch to their eye level; this is when you tell them you want them to stay in the room but they have to meet your expectations and it is now their choice what will happen: one-to-one.

So what? ◀◀◀

Let's return to those previous questions and try to answer them.

» *What does 'expectations' even mean?* In my humble opinion, it is just one rule that you consistently abide by (the one-voice rule).

» *How do you create a culture of high expectations?* From day one, carefully introduce and teach behaviour, rather than expecting it, founded in that human-first caring approach.

» *How does being a human-first teacher help?* Because all pupils find it harder to misbehave when they can see your investment in them.

» *How does this link to cognitive science?* Keeping it simple means you can use your cognition to be more aware of what is going on in terms of learning rather than being fraught with anxiety about behaviour management: the one-voice rule backed up by the behaviour policy.

» *And how can all of this empower you?* Because being rigid in your expectations means much more learning will happen in your classroom, and that is the fun part.

Classroom reflections

The hard truth is: sometimes it won't go well. There are times when I worked so hard to reach a pupil and thought it was cracked because last lesson they behaved and produced excellent work. Yet this lesson they are unsettled, maybe even rude and surly. So what did I do? Exactly as before: adopting my human-first caring, empathetic, consistent approach but this time adding in that I know they can behave well, as they demonstrated this last lesson. If your school allows, let the pupil stand outside for a few minutes to reflect, then again tell them you want them to start work and what you expect: for example, 'three lines of work' to be completed when you return in three minutes. To contextualise, however, some behaviours signalling distress may mean the pupil needs to go for pastoral care outside with a teaching assistant or head of year. If this is the case, remember it is not your fault. Sometimes problems are too big for you to deal with alongside trying to teach the rest of the class.

Another scenario: despite my own advice, sometimes a pupil would upset me with their behaviour. Every lesson, no matter how kind and empathetic I was, how consistently I applied the behaviour policy, I found it really difficult to reach them. So, what did I do? In this scenario, I spoke to members of staff who may know them and their family really well: find out what they like if you can. And then catch them being good; ask questions they can answer or have a conversation after class where you show an interest in their interests. Explain to them how their calling out or other behaviour will affect others and see if they are even aware of this fact. And then the next lesson or the next day, as they come through the door establish a contract: 'we are going to have a good lesson today, aren't we?' Every lesson is a fresh start for both of you, a clean slate. Most importantly, again remember that poor behaviour is just communication and there are influences on our pupils that are huge and sometimes very much out of our control.

The next case study will consider the situation in which you have already been teaching your class but have not got off on the right foot with the behaviours you want to see. That's okay! You are just going to press reset and communicate this fully to the class alongside an explanation of why you are now going to implement your 'new' one-voice rule. It may take a week or two, as it may do even when you enforce the one-voice rule from the outset. But by keeping it simple, teaching and checking they know the rule (ask them!) and adhering rigidly to the school's behaviour policy, I promise things will improve.

Top tip ◀◀◀

Do not ask for a behaviour: *teach* it with a simple change in language. For example, if a pupil is calling out, say: 'Asha, do not call out as this is not respectful of others, thank you'. This is much more powerful than saying 'Asha, please do not call out'. And while we are here, a huge top tip is to learn all pupils' names as quickly as possible. Draw them on a seating plan if it helps. Being addressed by name is far more powerful than a pointy finger.

Top tip ◀◀◀

If a pupil is refusing to follow your instructions, ask them this: 'Can I be clear, are you refusing to (eg *move to another seat as asked*)?' Sometimes a child may not even be aware that they are refusing instructions, so by using the above phrase you are teaching them and also giving them a very clear choice and ownership over what is going to happen next.

Let's summarise and think about the structure to establish a culture of high expectations of behaviour.

1. After your introduction to a class, tell the pupils how excited you are to be teaching them and how teaching is your passion (alongside your other human-first strategies from the last chapter; cue the use of chalk pens).

2. Teach them your one-voice rule, alongside a 3-2-1 or a clapping call–response, and explain *why* you will use it to ensure they are learning well and how it demonstrates respect for each other and you.

3. Explain the behaviour policy and say you will use it because you care deeply about the learning of *all* pupils in your class and that pupils who do not behave well are taking learning time away from those who do behave well, which is not very fair. Think about how you will have a visual reminder (chalk pens on the window/on the whiteboard etc). Use the 'Can I just be clear, are you refusing to...' statement to further teach pupils they are misbehaving.

4. Repeat the above each lesson (pupils will forget!): how much you love teaching but that you will invoke your one-voice rule relentlessly and consistently.

Now sometimes in reality there will still be pupils, often a group of pupils in a class, who just can't meet your expectations. The next most powerful weapon in your arsenal is parental contact. This can be time consuming, but it really is worth it when you are at a dead loss. Tell the pupil you are going to contact home every Friday with a short report on how this week has gone and that you would very much like it to be a positive communication. When Friday comes, send the email phrased something like: 'Javier is great to have in my class. Unfortunately, this week he has not settled despite warnings and this has had a negative effect on not only his learning but the learning of others. Please can we work together to try and improve this so Javier can reach his full potential?' Or perhaps it would be: 'Previously Javier has been quite unsettled but I am so delighted that this week he has produced excellent work and I am really proud'. The power of positivity cannot be expressed enough and you will see a huge shift in behaviour. I cannot tell you the number of times I have emailed and had the response along the lines of: 'Thank you so much, that was so lovely to hear. We only ever get bad phone calls/emails from school and it was so wonderful to get a positive one'. The impact is far reaching and has a ripple effect (and will make you feel so happy you made the effort when you were shattered on a Friday). To further add to the power of positivity, use postcards, house points, pupil of the week or any other tool that catches pupils being good. See @DrKellyR on Twitter for Google Drive links.

Top tip ◀◀◀

Remember you can use the **GROW** coaching model to structure conversations when supporting young people in your care. Help them to be metacognitive and empower them to take control of whatever situation that may be leading to them not behaving. This will be a good tool for a primary class but also for pupils in your tutor group if you teach secondary age. **G**: what is your absolute **g**oal in my class in terms of your behaviour? How would it feel to reach that goal? **R**: what is your **r**eality now, how far are you from that goal? **O**: what **o**ptions do you have in order to take decisive steps; some will work, some won't. **W**: what **w**ill you do now? Get the pupils to write it down with you and commit to making either small or big changes in order to reach that goal. Sometimes these break-time conversations with a child who is not behaving well can really flip things around.

Now what? ◀◀◀

Practical ways to implement this in your classroom: tomorrow, next week, next year

Practical task for tomorrow ◀◀◀

- This chapter has explored how to establish high expectations and some practical ways to implement them in your classroom. Answer the following questions and have a self-conversation about your next steps so that you are ready to GROW.

  - **G** – What is your *goal* in terms of behaviour management? What would it look like if all pupils are behaving? What would it feel like to know you have maximised learning by minimising displays of poor behaviour?

  - **R** – What is your *reality* now? Have you struggled to establish good behaviour routines? Can you examine why that might be? Has founding behaviour management on human-first approaches switched your thinking?

  - **O** – What are your *options*? Look back at the top tips and your notes to help you reflect on practical strategies that will support you to establish routines and teach the behaviour you expect. Which ones could you do?

  - **W** – Commit. Which ones *will* you do? Can you think of any others? Write down a statement that says: 'In my classroom I will... to ensure I combine human-first approaches with rigorous behaviour management'. Most importantly here, keep it simple so you can keep your mind clear for the purpose of actually teaching.

- Look at your 'I will' list and choose one or more you can implement quickly, whether it is with your class(es), your tutor group or a group of pupils for whom you are responsible. Plan it now: if it is something you are going to say to them, write down a 'script' and practise what you want to convey.

Practical task for next week ◀◀◀

Think about a pupil, a group of pupils or a class that you have been struggling with. How has implementing the strategies changed how they are behaving? Which ones are effective? Examine which ones do not work for you. If you are finding it really hard to settle pupils even with a 3-2-1 or the clapping response, tell the pupils you are going to use a timer to deduct time back from them. Start your timer when you have counted down or clapped and start to note on a sticky note who is still talking. When it is break time, if your school allows, keep those pupils back and spend time again teaching them why it is important to have one voice when you are in a teaching episode. Tell them it will be a fresh start next lesson.

Practical task for the long term ◀◀◀

To start with, keep it simple in terms of establishing routines; your one-voice rule embedded in human-first teaching backed up by your school's behaviour policy. Once you have established this, take a look at the Google Drive: what templates in terms of capturing good behaviour could you use? Star of the week? A display? A postcard? Choose one and try it with a class. Importantly, reflect on its impact: I am sure it will be purposeful but if it is not, refine your approach and try something new!

Reflective task ◀◀◀

- Do you have a new-found or deeper understanding of what high expectations are and how to establish them? Do you feel more confident with a simple strategy to follow? Mark your scale bar again. Hopefully it is further on than at the start of the chapter.

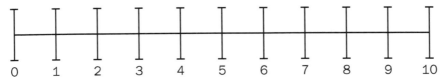

0   1   2   3   4   5   6   7   8   9   10

What next? ◀◀◀

Chapter 2 highlighted the importance of showing young people that you care not just about their learning, but about them as individuals. This chapter has built on that and shown that high expectations facilitate good learning environments. You will get to put this into practice the next time you step into a classroom, whether you are just observing or teaching. It will take time, but you will see the benefits. Use your list of 'I will...' to ensure you implement the practical strategies suggested or ones of your own. Below are some suggested links to further reading about how great expectations and teaching behaviour are fundamental.

Now it is time to really get stuck into the practicalities of using research-informed methodology to plan and teach great lessons. Let's do this!

Further reading

Chartered College of Teaching blog: Dix, P (2020) [online] Available at: https://earlycareer. chartered.college/behaviour-management-in-the-classroom (accessed 6 September 2021).

Chartered College of Teaching webinar on behaviour (the CCT has free membership for trainee teachers): Chartered College of Teaching (2020) Webinar: Behaviour Management Q&A – Tom Bennett and Amy Forrester. [online] Available at: https://my.chartered.college/ 2020/09/webinar-behaviour-management-qa-tom-bennett-and-amy-forrester (accessed 6 September 2021).

FutureLearn course on Behaviour for Learning: FutureLearn (2021) Managing Behaviour for Learning. [online] Available at: www.futurelearn.com/courses/managing-behaviour-for-learning (accessed 6 September 2021).

Great Teaching: The power of expectations: Sherrington, T (2018) Great Teaching: The Power of Expectations. Teacherhead. [online] Available at: https://teacherhead.com/2018/09/02/ great-teaching-the-power-of-expectations (accessed 6 September 2021).

References

Bennett, T (2010) *The Behaviour Guru* (1st ed). London: Bloomsbury.

Bennett, T (2020) *Running the Room: The Teacher's Guide to Behaviour.* Melton, Woodbridge: John Catt.

Dix, P (2017) *When the Adults Change, Everything Changes: Seismic Shifts in School Behaviour* (1st ed). Bancyfelin: Independent Thinking Press.

Chapter 4   A toolkit for lesson planning

What? (The big idea)

Planning cognitive science informed lessons will make you a great teacher

So far, this book has considered what cognitive load theory and cognitive science are, what being a human-first teacher entails, and in Chapter 3 how to stand confidently in front of 30 young people. You are now ready to begin the prodigious task of planning lessons. Naturally, some people appear more creative and some of your peers may seemingly be able to effortlessly plan amazing lessons. But let me reassure you that, at least at first, most early career teachers will spend two hours plus planning a one-hour lesson, which is unsustainable in terms of workload and well-being. The aim of this chapter is to break down the planning process into small steps and consider the elements that all good lessons should contain, while not overloading you cognitively or practically. By the end of this chapter, you will have a go-to toolkit of ideas which apply the principles of cognitive load theory, meaning you can confidently and efficiently plan lessons that will have a large impact on the pupils you are teaching.

- In pencil, mark on the scale bar your confidence in planning lessons. Again, the higher the number on the scale, the better you feel your planning is. (And yet again, don't worry whether you're a zero or an eight; the idea is that the chapter will shift your thinking. It's always about those +1s, or even +0.1s.)

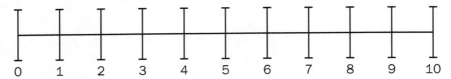

0   1   2   3   4   5   6   7   8   9   10

To a seasoned teacher, planning 'good' lessons is reminiscent of judgements made by either a senior member of staff or even Ofsted; it is shrouded in the relief of 'thank goodness it was okay' but also the disappointment of 'why wasn't it outstanding?' Thankfully, lesson gradings are now becoming a relic of the past. So, in the context of this book, a 'good' lesson is merely a proxy phrase for a lesson where pupils have made progress with knowledge, skills and understanding. In the curated Google Drive (see @DrKellyR on Twitter for the links) there are many templates to support you in planning; please feel free to use these however you would like to.

Reflective task ◀◀◀

- What elements do you think a good lesson should contain? List three or four important components.

Top tip ◀◀◀

At the heart of your planning, keep this in mind: *Precisely* what do you want pupils to know, and how will you know that they know it?

So what should be considered to build a good lesson?

Using the principles of cognitive load theory, it is possible to plan lessons across all age phases using the following structure.

1. How to begin: retrieval practice.

2. Time to get chunky: how to introduce new material in small steps.

3. How do you know what they know? Assessment in all its beautiful forms.

4. Knowing your pupils really well, data and beyond.

The first two strands are tackled in this chapter, the latter two in Chapter 5.

How to begin: retrieval practice (Why? How? What?)

The first question of 'why' you should do retrieval practice has been answered in Chapter 1 and through the reflective tasks in Chapters 2 and 3. Revisiting ideas and igniting thinking in your pupils transfers knowledge from the limited working memory to the infinite long-term memory. Remember: teaching happens in time and learning happens over time. So, while we are trying to plan good lessons where pupils make progress, I am reticent to say they will have 'learned' new skills or knowledge. If you plan your lessons carefully, the best you can hope for is that pupils have 'learned it for now'. You must remember that your pupils are switching between several different subjects per day, meaning that the knowledge you taught in the morning may be replaced in the working memory by the afternoon! So, you need to activate thinking and revisit ideas again and again until you are confident transference to the long-term memory has been achieved.

Beginning a lesson with retrieval practice has another huge added bonus. If you establish retrieval practice as part of your teaching routine, it will settle pupils and get them in the right frame of mind for the lesson you are teaching.

Case study ◀◀◀

I have seen hundreds of lessons where teachers have a PowerPoint slide labelled 'retrieval practice' which asks the pupils two or three questions based on the lesson they did the day before. The teachers put this slide in as they knew they should be doing retrieval practice due to a CPD session they had at the start of term. They are also aware that senior members of staff might check they were doing it. Despite how good the CPD may or may not have been, the teachers forget that learning happens over time and ideas need to be revisited frequently to embed them. Furthermore, many of these teachers cite worry over covering their curriculum to explain why they don't give sufficient lesson time to recalling previous topics.

Reflective task ◀◀◀

- What do you think is really important to include in retrieval practice? (Think, then check back to Chapter 1.)

- What should you say to the pupils about why they are doing it?

- Think of one positive and one negative about the observations in the previous case study.

One positive would be that pupils are reflecting back on previous learning. However, even for those pupils who can remember the learning the next day, a large proportion may forget it in a week's time. Remember from Chapter 1 that retrieval practice needs to encompass spaced practice and interleaving.

Spaced practice is where you leave a period of time when you think pupils have learned something and then revisit in two weeks or so to see if they still remember. This is my favourite part of retrieval practice! Pupils will pull all sorts of faces and make all sorts of noises. This is because they know the information but trying to retrieve it from long-term memory takes effort. But then you get the 'I've got it!' lightbulb moments, which are just magical, particularly when a pupil has really struggled with a concept or idea but suddenly realises that they have learned it.

Next, for an example of what interleaving might look like, consider the following two short lists of questions.

Finding percentages of quantity.

1. Find 10% of 200.

2. Find 50% of 600.

3. Find 15% of 240.

4. If 20% is equal to 5, what is the whole?

Attempt these questions.

1. $0.28 + 17.6$

2. $\frac{1}{4} \times 7$

3. 20% of 350

4. $3489 \div 17$

The first list would be good questions to do in a lesson when you have taught finding percentages and are looking to see how far you might challenge pupils by increasing difficulty. Would they be good questions for retrieval practice? Perhaps if you taught algebra a while ago and really want to see if the pupils can still do it, but compare these questions to the second list. This list has questions which are interleaved, leading to more thinking being activated as the pupils bounce from topic to topic. The idea is that you will give deeper learning if you revisit and recheck material from the last lesson, last week, last term and maybe even last year. Really solidifying knowledge of fractions or rounding or algebra gives strong foundations on which you can build concepts of ever-increasing challenge, because the links and schemas in your pupils' minds will be robust.

Now think about what you should say to your pupils. As covered in Chapter 1, be totally explicit in the 'why' – not just at the beginning of the year but continually throughout. Remember from Chapter 1 the protocol for introducing the rationale where you challenged your pupils to remember a list of 20 letters and digits, then asked them to write/say the lyrics of their favourite song or nursery rhyme? A reminder that memory is the residue of thought. Also, it is really important to convey to your pupils that retrieval practice is low-stakes assessment. It is merely a way for you to gather information about what they are remembering and what you need to re-teach; it is totally okay to get things wrong, as long as they ask questions and keep trying. See the table below for some dos and don'ts of retrieval practice.

Table 4.1 Some dos and don'ts of retrieval practice

Dos
Do as frequently as possibly (every lesson!).
Do explain to your pupils why they are doing retrieval practice.
Do include questions pertaining to the last lesson, last week(s), last term(s), last year (interleaving).
Do ensure you know who is getting which ones right or wrong as you go through the answers (reminding them that this is low stakes!). A quick hands-up as you go through each question will generate that data for you (more about this later).
Do include questions that were previously challenging but your pupils seemed to have mastered a couple of weeks or more ago (spaced practice).
Do be reassured that you will still cover your curriculum because your pupils' foundational knowledge will be so much stronger that they will assimilate new knowledge more easily.
Do explain, particularly to younger pupils, what 'retrieval' and 'practice' mean.

Don'ts
Don't just include questions from the last lesson.
Don't forget to check who got what right or wrong! How do you know whether they are mastering content if you just ask how many they got right out of a total out of 5 or 10?

Reflective task ◄◄◄

- Think about an upcoming lesson you are planning and write five questions that you could start the lesson with based on the above.

- What will you say to the pupils when you show the slide or give them the slip of paper with the questions on? Write this on your plan and take roughly five minutes to do this.

- Keep this 'lesson plan' in front of you so you can add to it as we go through sections 2 to 4 of planning.

Top tip ◄◄◄

There is no right or wrong format for retrieval practice, although many templates and resources are available to use. My advice is to just keep it simple: think about *your* class and simply write a list of questions based on your knowledge of them using the dos and don'ts above.

In summary, the process of retrieval practice is as follows.

1. Plan your questions.

2. Give the questions one at a time and tell pupils that it is not a test but practice in order to learn long term; to be completed in silence and without looking back in books.

3. Pupils can self-mark, or swap with a partner to mark (at your direction).

4. As you go through the answers, ask for a quick hands-up of who got that question right, again re-iterating you are just working out if you need to re-teach and what has been learned. In your planner just make a note of the rough number, eg 1/30, 16/30.

5. Following on from this, do not make it a data collecting exercise: make a judgement for each question which indicates either:

   a. none have remembered: do a quick re-teach;

   b. about half have remembered: tell them you'll include a similar question next time;

c. most have got it: leave for a couple of weeks and then recheck. In this category, for those that are still unsure, spend a couple of minutes with them at an opportune moment, for example when you set the class off on some independent work.

6. If they did get it wrong, pupils need to record the correct answer to help them to remember next time.

So what? ◀ ◀ ◀

You are trying to help pupils transfer their learning into their long-term memories. Starting a lesson with retrieval practice that has considered the learning needs of your class is an essential first step of a good lesson and is Rosenshine's first principle (Rosenshine, 2012). Remember that Rosenshine built his cognitive science principles on research-informed evidence. You will reap the rewards not just in the academic progress of your pupils, but in sharing in their success and increased confidence, which is priceless. It also links back to those pupils whose mindset is fixed: with practice you can prove the opposite.

Reflective task ◀ ◀ ◀

Retrieval practice for you.

- Write three strategies you can use in your classroom to convey your human-first teaching approach (think first and then flick back if you need to).

- What is the one simple rule that you are going to have in your classroom to maintain high expectations? (Again, flick back if you need to.)

You have now planned the start of your lesson: the review of previously taught content. Next, you will move to the introduction of new learning.

Time to get chunky: how to introduce new material in small steps (Why? How? What?)

Reflective task ◀ ◀ ◀

- For the lesson you are going to teach, where does it sit in a sequence of learning? What came before and what is coming next? Does the sequencing make sense to you?

In most schools, there will be schemes of work (or schemes of learning) which have a carefully planned order in which topics or subjects should be taught at each key stage. Often there is a spiral curriculum, where topics taught in earlier years are revisited and built upon in later years. This is because sequencing of learning is essential; for example, there is no use teaching the circulatory or reproductive systems without pupils knowing the structure and functions of cells. Or there is no point trying to introduce complex reading without a secure foundation of synthetic phonics. As an early career teacher, you are likely to be teaching in a school where the sequencing of lessons has already been mapped out by experienced teachers. But it is still worth considering the sequencing of lessons you teach in order to understand precisely what you want your pupils to learn.

Case studies ◀◀◀

For Year 5/6 learning relative clauses in grammar, you would have to atomise this into precisely what you want your pupils to know and what you are assuming they know already. In this example, pupils would have previously been taught:

1. what a clause is and how to recognise a subordinate and a main clause;

2. the difference between an object, a subject and a verb in a sentence;

3. punctation, including how comma pairs can be used for parentheses;

4. what pronouns are.

This is the precise prior learning atomised. In terms of sequencing, this needs to be secure in order to move on to the new learning around relative clauses. The precise new learning that you would want pupils to know is:

1. what a relative clause is and where it can be used in a sentence;

2. what a relative pronoun is;

3. how some relative clauses are embedded clauses and vice versa.

When writing precise learning points (PLPs), do not use phrases such as 'to understand...' This is vague and not measurable. Also, share the precise learning points with your pupils to make their learning journey explicit. Here are some examples for the carbon cycle for a Year 8 class:

1. Carbon dioxide is removed from the atmosphere by photosynthesis and by being dissolved in the oceans.

2. Carbon dioxide is released into the atmosphere by respiration and combustion.

3. Carbon in plants is passed on to animals when they eat the plants or other animals.

4. The carbon cycle shows the movement of carbon and carbon-containing compounds between the earth and the atmosphere.

5. Fossil fuels are non-renewable. They form from fossilised plants (coal) and microscopic animals (oil and gas).

Reflective task ◀◀◀

- Think about a lesson you are about to teach and get really precise about what you want your pupils to know. List three essential things. Take three minutes to do this and add it to the lesson plan you have started.

- Identify the precise prior knowledge your pupils need, as shown above.

- How will you check they have the prior knowledge to understand this new content?

You have now atomised the learning and have a clear idea of what precisely you want your pupils to know. Now, 'introduce new material in small steps, checking for understanding at each stage' (Rosenshine, 2012, p 13). Teacher exposition and explanation are absolutely key to make sure your pupils are learning, as long as you check for understanding at each stage. The key here is modelling. This underpins exactly how you are going to teach. It can be encompassed by the 'I do, we do, you do' mantra, so let's examine some strategies for this.

Remember dual coding from Chapter 1? In your arsenal of teaching tools, a whiteboard is a key piece of equipment. If it is paired with a visualiser, even better, as you will be facing your class.

Example ◀◀◀

Returning to the example of the carbon cycle and how this could be taught using dual coding, on the left is an image you would draw on your whiteboard for the class to see and in the boxes are your teacher exposition points. You can see that the diagrams are additive, with only a small piece of information being added at each step, thus not overloading the working memory.

Figure 4.1 How to dual code

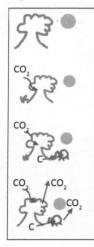

	Plants use energy from the sun to make their food source (glucose); this process is called photosynthesis.
	As part of the process of photosynthesis, plants take in carbon dioxide gas from the atmosphere to make the glucose. The carbon from the carbon dioxide thus becomes contained in the plant.
	Animals eat the plants and some of this carbon then goes into the animals to build their bodies. This is another way the carbon is cycled.
	Another way carbon is cycled is via the process of respiration, which all living organisms do. Respiration releases energy from glucose and the waste products are water and carbon dioxide, which get released back into the atmosphere.

This is an incomplete carbon cycle, but I hope you get the idea. Prior knowledge would have been an understanding of the processes of photosynthesis and respiration, so the sequencing is carefully considered. The new information is introduced in small steps, adding to the drawing slowly as you give your teacher explanation. Historically, teachers would have just showed the whole carbon cycle and explained it bit by bit, but pupils' attention would be all over the place, looking at the pictures, not attending to the right part of the diagram at the right time, reading while you were explaining, all in all contributing to information overload.

Top tip ◄◄◄

As you dual code, you *must* invite dialogue with your class. Tell them to ask you to re-explain at any point when they lose understanding.

Dual coding can be used across all age phases and subjects; and you do not need to be good at drawing! You can use it in maths or science to model a worked example; you can use it in history lessons to construct timelines and show how events link; in a geography lesson to show features of a landscape – the possibilities are endless. See the further reading section for some excellent videos on dual coding in action.

Using the visualiser and mini whiteboard to model and introduce new material in small steps is not limited to dual coding. If you are writing a paragraph in English, or analysing a text, having it displayed to the class to model how you would annotate and create is excellent teaching. Imagine you were going to model how to write a persuasive text; you can narrate your thinking and model metacognition as well as the skill. You can model how to make mistakes, change your mind, re-draft, all with a narrative which explicitly shows pupils how to approach the task. If you are doing a practical lesson, such as PE, DT or computer science, then modelling and 'I do' is implicit in a demonstration. Just encourage that dialogue and asking of questions!

Reflective task ◀◀◀

- You have written your retrieval practice questions and your precise learning points. Now consider how you can introduce these precise learning points: how are you going to model the knowledge or skill in small steps as described above (the 'I do')? Take five minutes to write a script and add it to your lesson plan.

Next to the 'we do'. You have done some exposition; now you need to see what pupils have understood by attempting something together. There are many approaches and what follows are just some suggestions. Importantly, whatever the 'we do' part contains, remove some of the support and assess whether pupils are ready to move on to some independent practice.

If it is a piece of writing, you can wipe your example off and invite the pupils to help you construct the next one, discussing all the elements that need to be included. For a history timeline, you could wipe it off and use questioning to facilitate pupils in reconstructing it. Alternatively, you could ask all pupils to write down a question pertaining to the teaching you have just done. They then share their question with their partner and decide which is the best to ask. You might then take four or six questions from the class that help you navigate what they found difficult to understand and even reveal misconceptions to you. In a PE lesson, you might have demonstrated a skill; the 'we do' bit is you and the class all practising together and you observing their levels of competency and correcting as they do so.

Reflective task ◀◀◀

- Reflect on how to address the 'we do' bit. Take two minutes and write it on your lesson plan.

Now it is time for your pupils to independently practise the new skill or apply the new knowledge: 'you do'. This is the opportunity for your pupils to solve equations, answer questions about the topic, write a paragraph, attempt that PE skill. But just before you set them off, get one or two pupils to repeat back to you what they are supposed to do, bounce it around the classroom if necessary; or invite them to ask you questions for clarity about what is expected of them.

Top tip ◀◀◀

During the 'we do' part of the lesson, you will have picked up on some pupils who are not grasping what you are trying to teach. Set yourself up at the front of the room at your 'help desk' and invite those struggling pupils to join you once you have set the others independent work. Let them explain what parts they didn't understand, provide the support and let them peel off to join their independent peers as they feel confident enough to tackle the work. Once you have all pupils working independently, rotate the room and give live feedback to support and challenge.

Silence is golden

What do you think of pupils working in silence on a task? What would hold you back from insisting on ten minutes of absolute concentration on the task? What could you do to switch that thinking? If you have worked hard on culturing the human-first teaching environment, have been rigorous in your implementation of the 'one-voice' rule and use of your school's behaviour policy, and explain that a short ten-minute silent activity will allow your pupils to produce the best piece of work they can, you will find their outputs really increase. You can still rotate around the room very quietly offering support and checking, but it is much harder for pupils to avoid work in this silent atmosphere, particularly if your modelling and structure have built up to this independence.

Top tip ◀◀◀

Use online timers to help you time bound activities. This adds pace and focus. But keep a level of flexibility because teaching is an art, dependent on so many factors, and cannot be fully planned down to the minute.

- Plan the 'you do' element. How are your pupils going to independently practise what they have been taught? Take five minutes to plan this; glance back at some of the top tips to help.

The most important thing in your planning, which should be easier when you have atomised the learning, is modelling the 'I do, we do, you do' approach. Keep this at the heart of your lesson planning, with the 'I do' part given over to you, as the expert in the room, to teach the content or skill.

Now what? ◀ ◀ ◀

Practical ways to implement this in your classroom: tomorrow, next week, next year

- Answer the following questions and have a self-conversation about your next steps so that you are ready to GROW.

  - **G** – What is your *goal* in terms of planning lessons? What would it look like if all of your lessons were good? What would it feel like to know you have maximised the outcomes of your pupils without spending hours at a cost to your work–life balance?

  - **R** – What is your *reality* now? Are you spending hours planning with variable outcomes? Are you trying to constantly come up with activities that engage your pupils or has your focus been absolute precision about what you want your pupils to know and how you will know that they know it?

  - **O** – What are your *options*? Look back at the top tips and your notes to help you reflect on practical strategies that will support you to plan your lessons efficiently.

  - **W** – Commit. Which ones *will* you do? Can you think of any others? Write down a statement that says, 'When I plan lessons I will...'

- Look at your 'I will' list; choose one or more you can implement quickly.

Practical task for next week ◀◀◀

Pick a methodology from the above and use it in all of your lessons next week. For example, you might decide that all lessons will involve mini whiteboard work for assessment, or that you will use a visualiser to dual code.

Practical task for the long term ◀◀◀

Keep what works; ditch what doesn't. Over time, keep reflecting back on your notes and the top tips, otherwise you are going to forget them.

- Evaluate how the retrieval practice is going (does it still adhere to the dos and don'ts above?).

- Evaluate how the modelling is going. Remember to use the 'I do, we do, you do' methodology when you are introducing new material.

Reflective task ◀◀◀

- Do you have a new-found or deeper understanding of how to plan lessons? Do you feel more confident? Mark your scale bar again to see your progress.

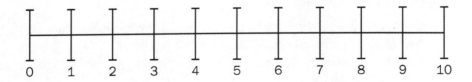

What next? ◀ ◀ ◀

This chapter has unpicked lesson planning and broken it down into elements to include in every lesson to ensure your pupils make progress. The next chapter will add some layering and examine how to use assessment to inform your planning, as well as how to plan to ensure that all of your pupils are making progress. Good luck with your planning!

Further reading

Adam Boxer modelling dual coding for ResearchED: ResearchED (2020) Adam Boxer: Dual Coding for Teachers Who Can't Draw: Teacher's Explanations. [online] Available at: www.youtube.com/watch?v=16SBht2iF_k&t=156s (accessed 6 September 2021).

Dual coding for teachers: Seneca (2021) Dual Coding for Teachers. [online] Available at: https://app.senecalearning.com/classroom/course/9375f141-2704-49d8-a754-e142c7aad967/section/3ed336fc-89f0-4dba-b853-4c9f61a0d3ed/session (accessed 6 September 2021).

Oliver Caviglioli modelling dual coding: ResearchED (2020) Oliver Caviglioli: Dual Coding to Organise Ideas. [online] Available at: www.youtube.com/watch?v=vsKBWsW2Unw (accessed 6 September 2021).

See the Twitter feeds of these teaching and learning experts:

@teachertoolkit: No 1 Education Blog UK.

@ensermark @impactwales: materials around whole-class feedback.

@katejones: materials and links to her books around retrieval practice.

@dylanwiliam: all things education-related.

Reference

Rosenshine, B (2012) Principles in Instruction: Research-based Strategies That All Teachers Should Know. *American Educator*, Spring: 12–39.

Chapter 5 Planning and assessment: knowing your pupils and knowing what they know

What? (The big idea)

Getting a real handle on assessment and how to plan for progress for all

Chapter 4 saw you start to plan lessons with purposeful retrieval practice and then how to introduce new material in small steps, checking for understanding at each stage. This is the first part of assessment. But assessment is so much more than that. It is married to feedback in all its guises and, coupled with knowing your pupils really well, is one of the best ways to maximise the progress of your pupils. The aim of this chapter is to give you go-to strategies that you can start to use straightaway for assessment and then to help you consider how to cater for the differing factors that might affect how well your pupils learn. The idea is to keep your cognitive load low, so remember to use your notebook to jot down the tasks and ideas as you go. By the end of this chapter, you will have a go-to toolkit of ideas which apply the principles of cognitive load theory, meaning you can confidently and efficiently plan lessons that will have a large impact on all the pupils you are teaching.

- In pencil, mark on the scale bar your confidence in how to formatively assess your pupils. In a different colour, mark how well equipped you feel to cater for all the factors that may affect the progress of your pupils. Again, the higher the number on the scale, the better you feel your planning is. (And yet again, don't worry whether you're a zero or an eight; the idea is that the chapter will shift your thinking. It's always about those +1s, or even +0.1s.)

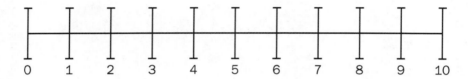

Parts 3 and 4 of planning a good lesson follow, this time layering in those important elements that help you support all your pupils to learn (for Parts 1 and 2, see Chapter 4).

How do you know what they know? Assessment in all its beautiful forms (Why? How? What?)

Remember the start of Chapter 4 when it was suggested that all good lessons can be distilled down to precisely what you want your pupils to know and how you know they know it? There are many books devoted to assessment because it is a vast topic, but this section of the book will give you some simple low-tech techniques that you can start using tomorrow. Formative assessment in these forms is often referred to as AfL (assessment for (or of) learning).

Let's start at the beginning, whether this is a new topic or a stand-alone lesson. The example in Chapter 4 of the carbon cycle was based on the sequencing of lessons that meant pupils already 'knew' photosynthesis and respiration. And the lesson on relative clauses required prior knowledge of what a clause and a pronoun are. If retrieval practice has been embedded successfully over a long period of time, you should be much more confident that this prior learning is secure. Regardless, before you begin your teaching exposition you need to ensure that the prior knowledge is sound. Here are some top tips on how to do this pre-assessment.

Top tip ◀ ◀ ◀

- Use the required prior knowledge as questions in your retrieval practice starter, re-teaching as necessary before the main part of the lesson.

- Give the whole class mini whiteboards and pens and question them: eg 'write the word equation for photosynthesis' or 'give two examples of pronouns'. All pupils can hold up their boards and show you what they know. Another top tip: *Everyone* has to hold their board up: it is non-negotiable. They can either write the answer, write the answer even if they are not sure, or put a '?' to show you that they do not remember. But everyone holds up their board, which you insist upon as you scan the room looking at the answers.

- Tell pupils to draw around their hand and in each finger write all they know about, say, photosynthesis and respiration or object/subjects/verbs in a sentence. Rotate the room and check.

- The lesson before you are going to start the topic, give a test-style question based on what you are about to teach and pre-assess it. Do not spend hours marking: just a quick read to see if they have any existing knowledge that you can build on. You can repeat the same question later on as a comparison.

- On a blank page in their books, ask pupils to write three facts and a question about the prior knowledge. Ask them to share the facts and the best questions with you so you can elicit what they know and re-teach if necessary.

Reflective task ◀ ◀ ◀

- Insert an arrow on your lesson plan between retrieval practice and the 'I do' sections and decide how you are going to know your pupils have the necessary prior knowledge. Take one minute to choose an approach from the top tips given above and write it down.

As you move to the 'we do' part of the lesson, you need to be able to assess how *all* pupils are getting on in readiness to move to the independent task.

Table 5.1 Some techniques you can use to achieve this

Strategy	How to do it
Mini whiteboards	Every pupil has a whiteboard and pen, and *all* pupils show you their responses at the same time.
Cold calling	You pose a question, leave thinking time and choose a pupil by name. You direct your questions to particular pupils to ensure that they are challenging 'enough' but not so much that they cause pupils to move into a panic state.
ABC questioning	You pose a question and choose, by name, a pupil to answer. Rather than respond to them yourself, invite other pupils to Accept, Build or Challenge the thinking. You can then facilitate a good discussion and address misconceptions.
Choral response	You pose a question, leave suitable thinking time and ask all pupils to respond in chorus.

Reflective task ◀◀◀

- What do you think some of the pros and cons of each technique are?

- Which ones would suit your style of teaching?

- How open are you to try one if you have not done so before?

Table 5.1 highlights four quick assessment techniques you can use to check for understanding. There are many more, but these are effective, everyday techniques.

Mini whiteboards

Method

1. Plan in whiteboard assessment to every lesson if you can.

2. Secure your whiteboard set and pens in the room(s) in which you teach.

3. Pose your question, leave wait time and then count down 3-2-1 when all boards are shown at the same time.

4. Scan and say things like 'yes, right, nearly there; try again using the example in your book' etc.

5. For a pupil who puts a '?', as previously discussed, ask someone who got it right to explain their answer. Then question again.

6. Are they ready to move on to the independent task? Do you need to re-model? Do you need to do another example? Are most pupils ready to move to independence so you can call the remainder to your 'help desk' as described in Chapter 4? Channel your responsive teaching.

Benefits

- You instantly have an insight into every pupil's thinking.

- This rapid quick-fire questioning will allow you to gather so much evidence for where your lesson needs to go next.

- You will establish who is ready to be independent so you can really expect them to be working when you set your timer, for say ten minutes. Therefore, it further acts as a behaviour management tool and a way to maintain high expectations: if they 'get it', as shown on their mini whiteboard, there is absolutely no reason not to attempt the given task. It also means you can manage the noise level during independence as they should all be concentrating on the task; this is where you can use those effective silent slots.

- Another upside of mini whiteboards is that some pupils quite like drafting on them before writing in their books, if they are quite particular about how their book looks. The ability to wipe off the boards allows some pupils who lack confidence in their thinking to try ideas out before committing to paper.

I cannot advocate enough the use of mini whiteboards as the best way to carry out formative assessment, informing you what pupils know and what their next steps should be.

Limitations

- You need to have a seemingly endless supply of pens because, despite how stringent you are in counting them in and out, they just seem to disappear.

- You are limited in how much pupils can write for you to feasibly scan quickly, so you will be limited to shorter answer questions. You have to get clever about how to break longer questions into shorter ones.

- Some teachers have a real worry that pupils will draw silly pictures, or doodle, or the boards will act as a distraction. I can honestly say this has never been an issue for me; teach the behaviour you expect: 'I only want to see answers to the question or a "?" on your board, anything else is not acceptable' or say, '3... pens and whiteboards all down, 2... look at me, 1... that's all, pens down and we are ready to move on', waiting silently until they have all followed this instruction.

Reflective task ◀◀◀

- How could you use mini whiteboards in the lesson you are planning? Take less than one minute to draw an arrow on your plan.

- Who could you contact in your school to secure you a class set of boards and pens?

Cold calling

This is a term first coined by Doug Lemov in *Teach Like a Champion* (Lemov, 2015) and has been rightly adopted by most teachers. The main premise is this: if you allow pupils to put their hands up when you are questioning, there is a good chance the same children who are confident will be the ones who raise their hands. How do you know what the quiet ones are thinking? How do you know the rest of the class did not zone out as soon as you started teaching, safe in the knowledge they did not intend to raise their hand so need not waste energy thinking about the learning? Cold calling, while still only allowing you to hear from one pupil at a time, allows you to direct your questions to a whole range of pupils.

Method

1. Pre-plan your questions with particular pupils in mind in terms of their challenge; this maximises trust and engagement.

2. Pose your question but add a pupil's name at the end of the question eg 'What is the difference between a noun and a verb, Hope?'

3. Leave thinking time (five seconds).

4. Allow your pupil to answer. Cultivate a culture of 'it is okay not to know, but it is not okay not to give your best try' to prevent 'I don't knows' (see below).

5. Probe for deeper thinking by asking a backup question such as 'Why?' or 'Can you now give me an example?' You can also choose to bounce this around with further cold calling.

You will have to reiterate, many times, that there are no hands up and you will eventually cultivate a climate where all pupils have to pay attention as they could be the one called upon at any time.

Benefits

>> All pupils will focus their minds on the learning because you might choose them to answer your next question.

>> You take away the luxury of a daydream and ensure pupils are focusing their minds on the learning. Sometimes you might even use a cold call when you notice a pupil is not paying attention, so it further acts as a behaviour management tool.

>> Cold calling gives you the opportunity to ask a wide variety of differentiated questions to a wide variety of pupils.

Naturally, despite how well you think you have taught something, you will get 'I don't knows' and often the wrong answer. It is really important to cultivate a classroom ethos where this is not allowed as a get out and you should then support the pupil to offer an answer. For example, if you posed the question: 'Which gas do plants need for photosynthesis... (five second gap), Pavel?' and Pavel replies: 'I don't know' or an incorrect answer such as 'Oxygen', you do not move on but ask further questions to support Pavel to get to the right answer, such as: 'Which gas do you rely on plants to produce so that you can breathe?'; 'Okay, so if the answer is oxygen, this can't be the gas plants need for photosynthesis because they produce it. What other gas is there in the air that plants could use?'

Fundamentally, all cold calling should be conducted in a kind, positive, supportive manner in the human-first way we explored in Chapter 2.

If a pupil gives a great answer then a level of challenge could be added in; or perhaps they give an answer which reveals a misconception. In these cases, follow up with: 'Why do you think that?' The 'why' question is a great questioning technique all in itself!

Limitations

>> You are unlikely to be able to hear from a whole class of 30 pupils during a cold call session, so there will potentially still be pupils who you cannot be sure have understood the learning.

If a pupil does reply, 'I don't know', tell them it doesn't matter if they are wrong but that they must have a go. 'What do you think the answer *might* be?' It is far better that they get it wrong as at least then you know where their thinking is – all done with kindness and positivity.

Reflective task ◀◀◀

- How could you use cold calling with your classes?

- Think about the shift in culture from hands up to no hands up questioning: what challenges will that pose for you?

- On your lesson plan, mark where you could use cold calling to check for understanding. What key questions will you ask? Give three minutes to do this.

ABC questioning

This is an extension of cold calling where, as stated above, you still pose a question, leave wait time and then ask a pupil a question.

Method

1. The difference is that when you receive a response from a pupil, you invite the other pupils to think about whether they Accept what has been said, want to Build on it, or want to Challenge it.

2. You then cold call another pupil to give their Accept, Build or Challenge.

3. You could allow your pupils to hold up their whiteboards with an A, B or C written on them so you can facilitate a really good debate and hear from a lot of pupils. Alternatively, they could hold up one, two or three fingers to Accept, Build or Challenge.

Benefits

» You get a fluid, dynamic discussion with a high engagement rate as the pupils are all having to listen to the responses from their peers and react accordingly. Importantly, you might find with these kinds of lessons that pupils are more likely to get excited and want to offer their opinions, so just be firm about teaching that one-voice rule.

Limitations

» The limitations are as above: you are still only able to hear from one pupil at a time but, again, it is still a great questioning technique.

Reflective task ◀◀◀

- On your lesson plan, do you think you could change cold calling to cold calling + ABC? Would that work for this lesson?

Choral response

Choral response is exactly what it says on the tin and is a great way to check for understanding of prior knowledge, or to repeat back instructions before starting independent practice. For example, if you had just done the dual coding with the carbon cycle as shown in Chapter 4, you could use choral response to fire questions. These could include:

» what is the process where plants make their own food source?

» what is the name of that food source?

» which gas do plants need in order to make the glucose?

» how does the carbon then get into animals? etc.

Method

1. Pose a question which has a defined answer that you have rehearsed with your class.

2. Ask your class to give you the answer in unison, all calling out the same answer at the same time.

3. Each time you pose a question, indicate with your hands or count down '3-2-1' for the response.

Benefits

>> It fires a nice energy into the classroom and does not depend on equipment to hear everyone's thinking.

>> You can scan the room and keep an eye on those who you think might be reluctant to answer; if they do not, then you can direct the question back to them and ask for their singular response.

Limitations

>> The biggest limitation is that you can only have very short answers; otherwise it would sound very messy!

Reflective task ◀◀◀

- Think of a lesson you are planning this week: it may be the one you're constructing right now, where choral response would be appropriate to trial.

As mentioned earlier, there are many questioning techniques to check for understanding but hopefully these four will give you a good repertoire of strategies to very easily apply to your classroom. As you progress through your career, you will refine, evolve and also create your own style. Questioning is an assessment technique to check for in-the-moment understanding; we will now move to feedback during or after the lesson.

Reflective task ◀◀◀

- What do you think is the best kind of feedback pupils can get?

- When should they get it?

- What should the feedback include? A grade, mark or percentage? A comment? Ways to improve?

Assessment and feedback during or after a lesson

The evidence around written feedback and its impact on pupil progress is weak. However, an evidence review overseen by the Education Endowment Fund summarises the factors that support pupil progress (Elliott, 2016).

- Verbal, in-the-moment, feedback is the best way to support a child to make progress.

- If you give a grade/mark/percentage, you direct the pupil's attention to their score and they will not focus on how to get better. Therefore, comment-only marking is preferable.

- Acknowledgement marking, eg the tick and flick on, have no effect on pupil progress and therefore waste a teacher's time.

- If giving written feedback, class time must be allowed for pupils to respond to that feedback. This is sometimes called DIRT (Directed Improvement and Reflection Time).

- When providing targets, whether verbal or written, the actions should be kind, specific and actionable. Not 're-write your paragraph but try harder'.

- Careless mistakes in a pupil's work should be highlighted but not corrected.

Marking written work, homework, test papers etc can be overwhelming for an early career teacher and you will be governed by your school's feedback policy on the expectations around this.

Top tip ◀◀◀

Talk to your mentor and find out the marking expectations of your department, if in secondary, or year group in primary. There are probably set pieces of work per term that you can focus on.

Top tip ◀◀◀

The more live marking you can do while your pupils are working independently, the more progress they will make. Circulating the class checking, intervening, advising and explaining precisely what your pupils need to do will have more impact than any piece of written marking done at a distance from the pupil.

Whole-class feedback has gained a lot of traction in recent years and there are many resources you can use (see the further reading section at the end of the chapter). Feedback sheets can cut marking a set of books down to half an hour but still have the same impact on progress. You only write on the sheet, while scanning the books and filling in the template below as you do. Common misconceptions can be addressed, next steps in terms of DIRT questions can be written, and spelling, punctuation and grammar errors can be recorded. The feedback sheet is then copied and given to each pupil to stick in their books and respond to in the allocated time. The polaroid moment box is to indicate those pupils' work which is exceptional and even worthy of a photograph. Other pupils can use 'polaroid moments' to see What A Good One Looks Like, often called a WAGOLL, or a model answer, sharing good practice among themselves. The boxes can be edited to suit your classes and context: for example, you may wish to take out the missing/incomplete work box if you feel this would have a detrimental effect.

Figure 5.1 An example of a whole-class feedback template

🛡 **Marking Crib Sheet**	Date _____	Class _____
Praise:	Missing/incomplete work:	SPaG errors:
Cause(s) for concern:	Misconceptions:	Presentation:
DIRT questions	◀ Actions:	
📑 Polaroid moments:		

Dylan Wiliam, as introduced in Chapter 1, is passionate about purposeful assessment that allows you to teach responsively, that is, change the roadmap of your plan based on the formative assessment you are doing with your pupils. I urge you to visit his website (Wiliam, 2012) or his YouTube channel (Wiliam, 2020). His particular passion is for diagnostic, or hinge, questions that can be asked quickly for you to judge your next steps. A hinge question would look something like this:

Which of the following are true?

A. Photosynthesis is where plants use oxygen to make glucose.

B. Respiration only happens in animals.

C. Plants and all other living things use the process of respiration to release energy from sugars such as glucose.

D. Plants take in carbon dioxide and release oxygen into the atmosphere when they photosynthesise.

Pupils would (hopefully) write C and D on mini whiteboards. The other two are common misconceptions or common errors that you have tried (if doing the lesson on the carbon cycle mentioned in Chapter 4) to address. The information would then determine where you should go next with the teaching. Do you need to do some reteaching, or some questioning, or practise to really cement that piece of learning? Hinge questions are great because they will quickly show the direction your lesson needs to take; however, it can be quite challenging to write good ones so this would be worth a discussion with your mentor.

Dylan also advocates peer and self-assessment. Here's what he has to say about peer assessment:

> Now, when we talk about peer assessment, a lot of people just assume we are talking about having kids marking each other's work so that the teacher doesn't have to do it, and people always get the wrong idea because that's summative peer assessment. What we've discovered is that formative peer assessment, where pupils are helping each other improve their work, has benefits for the person that receives feedback but also has benefits for the person who gives the feedback. Because, in thinking through what it is that this piece of work represents and what needs to happen to improve it, the pupils are forced to internalise a success criteria and they're able to do it in the context of someone else's work, which is less emotionally charged than your own. So, what we routinely see... we see very, very commonly is when pupils have given feedback to others about a piece of work, their own subsequent attempts at that same work are much improved because they're now much clearer about what good work in that task looks like. So, that's been one of the real, I think, breakthroughs... is the real benefit of peer and self-assessment, is both the person who is doing the assessment, the self-assessment and the person who is giving feedback – the peer assessment.
>
> (Wiliam, 2014)

So, peer assessment is having pupils assess another's work against a set of success criteria, which activates their thinking about their own piece of work and how to improve it. Self-assessment is where you are 'activating pupils as learners of their own learning' (Wiliam, 2014). For both, it is essential that the 'success criteria' have been clearly established with the class so they have a good understanding of what they should include. For example, in a lesson where the precise learning point is to 'Use a variety of language techniques to write a crime story', the success criteria for the 'You do' independent practice part of the lesson could be:

>> to use three powerful adjectives;

>> to use a simile;

>> to use three different sentence lengths for impact.

There is precision here, meaning all pupils can succeed. The pre-assessment will have ensured that pupils have a good understanding of each of these terms; the 'I do' and 'We do' will have modelled how to use them and then pupils write during the 'You do' in silence for ten minutes. After the ten minutes, it would be time for self- or peer assessment against these criteria, and this can be conducted in several ways.

>> Using highlighters of different colours to show where, for example, the simile is. The highlighting will show what is missing and what still needs to be added. If no highlighters or different coloured pens are available, just circling with a key will be as effective. Pupils can then all hold up their books so you can see how they are getting on and what to do next.

>> Using a Venn diagram: the model answer has these (written in the left-hand section of the Venn diagram); mine/yours has these features in common with the model answer or success criteria (to go in the crossover section of the Venn diagram); and the missing features are written in the right-hand side of the Venn diagram, indicating the next steps.

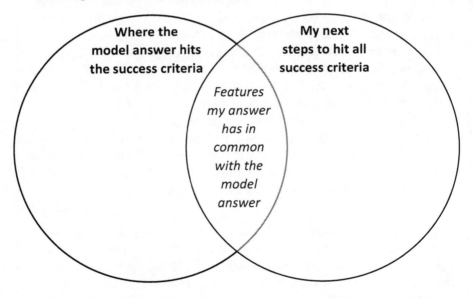

>> Pupils assess their or their peers' work against the success criteria and you bounce questioning around to give great examples of where/how specific criteria were included. This gives pupils ideas of what else they might include.

Again, this is not an exhaustive list but offers some easy starting points for you to try, refine and evolve.

Reflective task ◀◀◀

- On your lesson plan, highlight where you might be able to use one or more of the following to check progress during or after a lesson.
  - Live marking: rotating the room checking work, signposting and steering pupils.
  - Hinge point or diagnostic questioning.
  - Self-assessment.
  - Peer assessment.
  - Whole-class feedback sheets.
- Mark on your lesson plan how you will do this during the 'You do' part of the lesson or when you collect the work in. Take five minutes to consider the success criteria and how you will assess pupil progress.

Exit tickets

So far, we have discussed how to perform pre-assessment, how to check for in-lesson understanding and some strategies around marking and feedback.

Next to another one of my favourites: the exit ticket. Again, there are editable templates on the Google drive for you to use but an exit ticket could be a blank sticky note or small piece of paper; no fancy printouts are necessarily required! Exit tickets are used to finish off the lesson in order to really capture what the class have (for now!) understood. Every pupil has to write their name on their piece of paper so you know who knows what. The exit ticket could include:

» write three things you learned today;

» answer this question…;

» ask a question about something you learned today;

» ask a question about something you were unsure of;

» what is the most important thing you learned today?

There is no right, wrong or prescriptive way to do this simple exercise, but when planning your exit tickets, consider what you really want the children to have precisely learned and how you will know that they have learned this. To leave the class, or go to break/playtime, every pupil has to hand you their exit ticket to read. These should then give you an insight into what the pupils have grasped. Sometimes this can be very humorous as it becomes clear that you have *really* laboured a point, and will then act formatively in terms of your next steps in planning. The exit tickets can be handed back to pupils in the next lesson if you wish them to stick them in their books. Alternatively, you could just do questioning with mini whiteboards so you can see whether pupils have captured the learning; this will inform your planning for the next lesson.

Reflective task ◀◀◀

- On your lesson plan, write 'Exit ticket' and spend two minutes considering how you can capture your pupils' thinking. Refer to the previous top tip for ideas of questions.

Let's reflect on what makes a good lesson and your next steps

1. You have written your retrieval practice questions.

2. You have written your precise learning points.

3. You have planned pre-assessment and how to check for the prior knowledge needed for this lesson (mini whiteboards, cold calling, ABC, choral response).

4. You have planned how you are going to introduce new material in small steps ('I do').

5. You have planned the 'We do'; how you are going to model together the learning.

6. You have planned the independent practice ('You do') and considered some formative assessment around how you know the pupils are making progress.

7. You have considered the end of the lesson to capture whether you know what the pupils have actually 'learned' (exit ticket).

This is shaping up to be a good lesson. The final missing element is knowing your pupils really well so that you can cater for their differing needs.

Knowing your pupils really well, data and beyond (Why? How? What?)

As a teacher, you have to cater not only for different personalities and circumstances, but also for factors that may inhibit the progress of some of the pupils in your class or classes. Data about the pupils may tell us some basic information, but what if they are a pupil who excels in maths but struggles in English? Or is confident in one topic but is struggling with this one?

Differentiation is a broad term that encompasses planning your lesson so that all pupils, regardless of ability, background or circumstances, will make progress in your lesson.

Reflective task ◀◀◀

- Reflect on your own schooling; how well did your teachers know you? Did they know how to get the best out of you, and if so, how did they do that?

- What could they have done to help you more?

- Next, write down four things that might prevent a pupil in your class making as much progress as their peers.

Once again, this topic area is vast and worthy of a whole book all by itself. The needs of your pupils will not only have variation on paper in terms of their data, but also be influenced by a multitude of other factors that may change on a daily basis. The aim of this section is once again to give you some go-to strategies that you, as an early career teacher, can use while acknowledging they are not exhaustive. As you develop in your teaching, you will have the confidence, experience and even just the time to get to know your pupils really well. This will then allow you to refine and develop your own strategies or evolve existing ones.

Let's first look at some pupils who you can mark on your seating plan as those that might need extra checking in on or support. You can discuss with your mentor or access the school's data system to establish who in your classes may be considered one or more of these:

- pupil premium or disadvantaged;

- EAL (English as an additional language) where a language other than English is spoken in their homes;

- SEND (special educational needs or disabilities);

- those with lower previous attainment.

While the data is indicative of those who might need support, it is absolutely worth discussing your classes with your mentor and other expert colleagues in the school. For example, most schools will require you to know your pupil premium pupils and ensure you are catering for them. But while it is true that some pupil premium pupils will indeed require intervention, this is absolutely not true for all pupil premium pupils.

Top tip ◀◀◀

Turn that questioning over to the pupils again with another human-first bit of teaching: give all pupils a sticky note and ask them to tell you something that helps them learn or understand better (make sure they write their name on it). Tell them they cannot write 'working with my friends'!

As discussed in Chapters 1 and 2, most schools will have an agenda around 'closing the educational gap' between pupils from disadvantaged backgrounds and their peers. For some of those pupils, their home circumstances are unimaginable and there may be no suitable space for them to complete homework. Often, their chaotic home lives may have a huge impact in terms of their organisational skills (such as completing homework) and having the correct equipment (such as a pen and their book). This is certainly not true for all pupil premium pupils, and will also be true for some pupils who are not classified as pupil premium. But for those to whom it does apply, this is where your human-first teaching will come into its own. Showing your pupils you believe in them, that they are valued and are going to be successful in your lesson can be more than half the battle. Keep your expectations as high for them as for the rest of the class and support them to get there.

Reflective task ◀◀◀

- How can you support pupils who are disadvantaged with their readiness to learn? Could you keep a box of pens? Keep their book in class? Provide materials for homework such as paper or card?

Top tip ◀◀◀

Modelling of behaviours is really important here and it can start with a 'well-worn path'. This can be during questioning episodes or when pupils are working independently. Mark on your seating plan those pupils you need to 'visit', either verbally or in person, and make sure you follow this up in the lesson.

Pupils in your class may have specific special educational needs or disabilities. They could have dyslexia or autism spectrum disorder (ASD), be visually or auditorily impaired, have a physical need such as cerebral palsy, among many others. Some, but not many unless in a special needs school, will have an EHCP (education and health care plan). Some, but not many, may have assigned teaching assistants or learning support assistants. Where do you begin with supporting all of these pupils? A great place to start is the *SEND Code of Practice* (Department for Education, 2020), which you will be asked to sign as an early career teacher. You will also receive training on SEND in your training year and through your professional themes as an early career teacher.

Top tip ◀◀◀

You will receive a lot of general training around SEND but my top tip is that as soon as you have your class lists, arrange a meeting with your SENDCo (the special educational needs coordinator). Your SENDCo will know your pupils and their families inside out and will be able to tell you what works for them in class and how you can support them. The other meeting to book is with the teaching assistants or learning support assistants who are with your pupils and, again, know them really well and how to support good progress. This is a much more personal approach and will give you far more information than data held on your school's central system.

EAL and SEND: Practical strategies for your classroom

You will also receive training on how to support pupils who have English as an additional language (EAL). There can be a whole range of diverse languages and ability in English within your pupils classified as EAL so the advice is to speak to your SENDCo to glean as much information as you can about how to support your EAL pupils.

The great thing about the following strategies is that they will not only support your disadvantaged, SEND and EAL pupils, but will help all of your pupils learn better.

>> Glossaries or keyword lists at the beginning of a topic: get in the habit of ensuring that literacy skills are not a barrier to learning by providing these to all pupils and having them refer to them during lessons. For EAL pupils, you can give a translation of the keywords to further support their literacy.

>> Planning any written resources or presentations carefully with dyslexic pupils in mind: Arial or Comic Sans, using larger font and line spacing and using only bold for emphasis, not underlining or italics.

>> Planning your lessons (including any resources and presentations) with cognitive load theory in mind, eg including retrieval practice, introducing new material in small steps, modelling etc, as described above. Only include diagrams that add to the learning.

>> Plan your seating plan so pupils who need additional support are nearer the front with pupils who can actively model the learning sitting next to them or nearby.

>> Asking your pupils what works for them to help them learn best as described above and referring to it.

>> Having your 'well-worn path' where you visit pupils who need additional support first to ensure understanding and engagement.

>> Provide resources which scaffold tasks such as writing frames, sentence starters or structure strips to support those who need it.

Knowing your pupils is absolutely key. The bigger picture, ensuring all pupils make progress and having an understanding of factors that inhibit learning may take some time, but the previous list should give you a starting point.

Top tip ◄ ◄ ◄

For all pupils, high expectations of behaviour, their outputs and effort are key, but effort is what you should rate above all other things. Communicate this to your pupils.

Challenge with support

You should have come across the word differentiation, not just in reference to the groups above but for the differing abilities within your class. There was a recent fashion for learning objectives to be labelled 'All, Most, Some' or 'Bronze, Silver, Gold' with different levels of work or outcomes that pupils aim for.

- Imagine you are a child with SEND who really struggles with understanding and then completing tasks. How would it feel every lesson to know you will only ever be a bronze?

- Now imagine you are a high-achieving child. What effect might always completing 'gold' have on your mindset and your empathic skills?

If you teach using the cognitive science informed principles already discussed, and you share your precise learning points with your class, then *all* can be successful. Your modelling and introducing material in small steps methodology should mean that all pupils should be able to engage with their tasks. What you need to really think about is how you can ensure all pupils are challenged and then offer the support to those who need it (eg using the help desk approach mentioned earlier in the chapter). You do not need to write/print three different worksheets; again, this would give a burdensome workload. All you need to do is consider how you know your pupils have understood your precise learning points and then think about how you can extend the thinking of those who fly through.

Again, most schools will have improving differentiation as part of their school improvement plan and will expect to see 'Think Harder', 'Go Further' and 'Extension Task' readily visible. Whatever moniker is chosen, don't just pay lip service to it.

Reflective task ◀◀◀

- What is the purpose of the 'Think Harder' task? Really think about it.

- Who should do it?

- How will you know who has done it? Is it important to know?

After reflecting on these questions, add a challenging question to your lesson plan for those who might sail through the 'You do' part of the lesson. Think about who should attempt the challenge (you might have one or two names in your head who you can direct towards it, but keep it open for your formative assessment to dictate as the lesson unfolds). Then consider how you will *know* the pupils have completed it: a quick read is enough!

The last piece of advice is to keep a 'back-pocket' challenge for those who have sailed through the work and successfully completed the 'Think Harder' task. A simple idea is to write a challenging question for another finisher to complete. This taps into the often-competitive nature of more able pupils and often there are two in the class who can write questions for each other.

Reflect on what you have so far for a good lesson and your next steps

- You have written your retrieval practice questions.

- You have written your precise learning points.

- You have planned pre-assessment and how to check for the prior knowledge needed for this lesson.

- You have planned how you are going to introduce new material in small steps ('I do').

- You have planned the 'We do': how you are going to model together the learning.

- You have planned the independent practice ('You do') and considered some formative assessment around how you know the pupils are making progress.

- You have considered the end of the lesson to capture whether you know what the pupils have actually learned.

- Now plan in how you are going to cater for your vulnerable groups (do you need to change the seating plan? Make a glossary? Ensure there are textbooks available for them to refer to?). Spend five minutes doing this.

- Finally, look at the 'You do' section of your lesson plan. How could you really ensure there is challenge there? Add an extension task. Give three minutes to do this.

Now what?

Practical ways to implement this in your classroom: tomorrow, next week, next year

Practical task for tomorrow ◀◀◀

- Answer the following questions and have a self-conversation about your next steps so that you are ready to GROW.

  - **G** – What is your *goal* in terms of all pupils accessing the learning and you being aware of where they are in their learning journeys? What would it look like if all of your lessons had excellent assessment? What would it feel like to know you have maximised the outcomes of your pupils without spending hours at a cost to your work–life balance?

  - **R** – What is your *reality* now? Are you spending hours planning with variable outcomes? Are you trying to constantly come up with activities that engage your pupils or has your focus been absolute precision about what you want your pupils to know and how you will know that they know it?

  - **O** – What are your *options*? Look back at the top tips and your notes to help you reflect on practical strategies that will support you to plan your lessons efficiently.

  - **W** – Commit. Which ones *will* you do? Can you think of any others? Write down a statement that says, 'When I plan lessons I will...'

- Look at your 'I will' list; choose one or more you can implement quickly.

Practical task for next week ◀◀◀

Pick a methodology from this chapter and use it in all of your lessons next week. For example, you might decide that all lessons will involve mini whiteboard work for assessment or use exit tickets.

Practical task for the long term ◀◀◀

Keep what works; ditch what doesn't. Over time, keep reflecting on your notes and the top tips, otherwise you are going to forget them.

- Can you try a new questioning technique if you have successfully embedded one of those mentioned in this chapter?

- Evaluate if you really are challenging all pupils. Are you stretching the most able with your back-pocket task yet supporting those who struggle?

- Try the whole-class feedback sheet: plan it into a piece of work and see if it cuts your marking time down.

Reflective task ◀◀◀

- Do you have a new-found or deeper understanding of how to plan lessons where your assessment shows you that all pupils are making progress? Do you feel more confident? Mark your scale bar again to see your own progress.

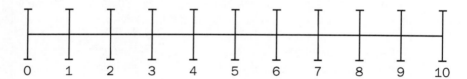

What next? ◀◀◀

The last two chapters have unpicked lesson planning and broken it down into elements to include in every lesson to ensure your pupils make progress. The next chapter will add some layering and examine how you can move from being hyper aware of your inexperience to gaining deep confidence.

Further reading

Assessment for teachers: Seneca (2021) Assessment for Teachers. [online] Available at: https://app.senecalearning.com/classroom/course/04e36b88-c9c6-47ac-8a4b-54b9ceeea532 (accessed 6 September 2021).

Chartered College of Teaching free resources around SEND, EAL, differentiation, assessment and planning for early career teachers: Chartered College of Teaching (2021) [online] Available at: https://earlycareer.chartered.college/?s=SEND; https://earlycareer.chartered.college/?s=EAL; https://earlycareer.chartered.college/?s=differentiation; https://earlycareer.chartered.college/?s=assessment; https://earlycareer.chartered.college/?s=planning (accessed 6 September 2021).

FutureLearn course on Assessment for Learning: FutureLearn (2021) Assessment for Learning: Formative Assessment in Science and Maths Teaching. [online] Available at: www.futurelearn.com/experttracks/formative-assessment-for-learning (accessed 6 September 2021).

FutureLearn course on differentiation: FutureLearn (2021) Differentiation for Learning. [online] Available at: www.futurelearn.com/courses/differentiating-for-learning-stem (accessed 6 September 2021).

The Learning Scientists discussing retrieval practice strategies: The Learning Scientists (2016) Study Strategies: Retrieval Practice. [online] Available at: www.youtube.com/watch?v=Pjrqc6UMDKM (accessed 6 September 2021).

References

Department for Education (2020) *SEND Code of Practice*. [online] Available at: www.gov.uk/government/publications/send-code-of-practice-0-to-25 (accessed 6 September 2021).

Elliott, V (2016) *A Marked Improvement? A Review of the Evidence on Written Marking*. [online] Available at: https://educationendowmentfoundation.org.uk/public/files/Presentations/Publications/EEF_Marking_Review_April_2016.pdf (accessed 6 September 2021).

Lemov, D (2015) *Teach Like a Champion 2.0* (2nd ed). San Francisco: Jossey-Bass.

Wiliam, D (2012) Dylan Wiliam's website. [online] Available at: www.dylanwiliam.org/Dylan_Wiliams_website/Welcome.html (accessed 6 September 2021).

Wiliam, D (2014) Self and Peer Assessment: Dylan Wiliam. [online] Available at: www.youtube.com/watch?v=5P7VQxPqqTQ (accessed 6 September 2021).

Wiliam, D (2020). What Every Teacher Needs to Know About Assessment. [online] Available at: www.youtube.com/watch?v=waRX-IOR5vE (accessed 6 September 2021).

Chapter 6   Next steps: consciously incompetent to unconsciously competent

What? (The big idea)

How to gain confidence and be the best you can

>> How do you balance your work and life and not get overloaded?

>> How do you focus your attention on how to drive your development forward?

>> When does it all get easier?

As a novice teacher, you will have undertaken observations of experienced teachers and wondered: 'How will I ever be like that and have that level of mastery?' I remember my mentor planning her lessons just by writing a lesson title in her teacher planner and being in awe of her. As an early career teacher, it is overwhelming trying to get to grips with a new profession. You have to learn to speak in the common teaching vernacular, peppered with acronyms; you have to plan lessons accounting for the needs of your different pupils; attend after-school meetings and training; and then find time to mark the work your pupils produce – as well as trying to live a home life, balancing time when you are not thinking about work.

Reflective task ◀◀◀

- In pencil, mark on the scale bar your personal awareness of how you can move your teaching forward without impacting on your work–life balance. The higher the number on the scale, the more positive you feel about both. (Again, don't worry whether you're a zero or an eight; the idea is that the chapter will shift your thinking. It's always about those +1s, or even +0.1s.)

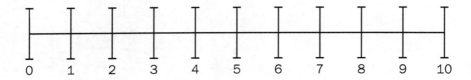

0   1   2   3   4   5   6   7   8   9   10

As an early career teacher, you are probably acutely conscious of your incompetency. This book, and the support of the expert colleagues around you, will start to move you towards a place where you become more consciously competent and get better at teaching. After a period of time, due to all of the practice you do, you will reach a stage where your working memory is free from the angst of the early career mindset and you become unconsciously competent. It is critical to point out here that this journey is certainly not linear, and all teachers will bounce back along the continuum many times. There are also certainly times when an early career teacher will be unconsciously incompetent. This chapter aims to reassure you that all you can do is your best, and focuses on how you can use a marginal gains approach to keep improving. Furthermore, it provides some quick strategies that can support your journey.

Reflective task ◀◀◀

Being reflective is the most important attribute a teacher can have.

- Consider how good you are at receiving feedback and consider the barriers to this. Could ego be a factor? Or your perception of the skills of the person giving you the feedback?

- What do you think is the purpose of reflecting on what went well and what your next steps might be?

- How can the expert colleagues around you best support this process of reflection?

When you have worked really hard on a lesson, perhaps spending more hours planning it than it took to deliver, it can be heartbreaking if it does not go well, or the feedback feels negative. But think back to your observations of expert colleagues and consider this: were all aspects of the lessons brilliant? Is there feedback you could give them to make it even better? The point is that the day you think you are a perfect teacher and do not need to get better is probably the day to stop teaching. The art of teaching is something you can get better at, but you are never 'done'. There are always new things to try, everchanging contexts to bring into the classroom and children whose needs are different to those you have encountered before. So, as long as you are self-aware and have an inner drive to continually get better for the sake of your pupils, then be kind to yourself. Accept the feedback for what it is: a way to help you improve. If you don't understand how to implement it or what your mentor means, then ask them to break it down into steps and model it to you. Do not be afraid to ask clarification questions. This is where the expert colleagues can really support you in your reflections and ensure you have a good understanding of what you need to do next. In terms of reflecting, it is powerful to first recognise the progress you are making and the aspects you are getting right, and then focus on the next steps.

Reflective task ◀◀◀

- In the Google Drive (see @DrKellyR on Twitter) is a spreadsheet titled 'Reflections', including all the 'learn that' and 'learn how to' statements from the initial teacher training Core Content Framework (CCF) and Early Career Framework (ECF). Download a copy. In the columns to the right of the 'learn how to' statements, type a number between 1 (I am not confident) to 10 (I have mastered this). Do this for each of the statements; it will take ten minutes or less.

This sheet is a tool to work out areas that you really need to work on at a granular level, but you can share it with your mentor if you like. There are many statements and you cannot hope to be '10' in all of them. You need patience and a marginal gains approach, working on one thing at a time to cement it before the next target is addressed. Really focus in on those around behaviour and relationship building because even if you plan an amazing lesson, the delivery will depend on your pupils being respectful and well behaved.

Reflective task ◄◄◄

Consider recording your lessons.

- What barriers are there to recording yourself teach? How can you overcome these and commit to it?

- What impact would it have on your progress and confidence to see how far you have come along the consciously incompetent to unconsciously competent continuum?

Look again at the spreadsheet and pick one or two areas that you think you need to work on and get granular with.

- What would it look like if this was 10 out of 10 on the mastery scale? Write three 'success criteria'.

- Where are you now on the scale of 1–10? What could you do to take it +1 or even +0.1?

- Who could support you in this process?

Top tip ◄◄◄

Send an email to the teachers in your school, inviting them to drop in on your lessons. Tell them what you are working on, eg questioning, and invite them to give you feedback. By being 10 per cent braver and having an open-door policy, you are accepting that you are a novice teacher with lots to learn and feedback can support that journey. Feedback is a gift.

Record your lesson

Recording one of your lessons can be for your eyes only, unless you want to share of course. You need to be 10 per cent braver again. You may initially find this embarrassing and for the first few minutes you will focus on your voice and how strange it sounds, or what you look like. That is completely normal. But what you will learn, once you are past the point of feeling uncomfortable, is incredibly powerful. For the purposes of safeguarding, please do make sure you follow your school's policy on recording lessons. Observing yourself, rather than having feedback from a colleague, will show you the following:

» how you project your voice and what your tone is like, your body language and even if you smile;

» whether your instructions are clear;

» where you stand in the classroom and which pupils you call upon;

» how you respond to pupils' questions and teach responsively;

» whether you have phrases or words that you overuse without realising;

» whether you are enforcing your one-voice rule.

The list is endless! By watching a recording of your lesson, you can really hone in on whether your granular +1 targets are being effectively addressed. You will also see lots of good practice, which will reassure you. It is one of the best professional development tools you can use and you will be pleased that you did it.

Case study ◀◀◀

Starting lessons

I supported an early career teacher who was missing that pupils were not starting tasks and she was not scanning the room checking for low-level disruption. With her mentor they talked about how to address this.

- Scan the room when giving instructions to ensure all pupils focus on you: use verbal or non-verbal communication to refocus pupils if necessary.

- Check that pupils have understood the task before they start on the independent practice.

These link to the following 'learn how to' statements.

- Checking pupils' understanding of instructions before a task begins.

- Giving manageable, specific and sequential instructions.

- Using consistent language and non-verbal signals for common classroom directions.

The mentor modelled how to do this with the early career teacher observing. They then practised together away from the classroom environment. Then the early career teacher was observed by the mentor putting it into action. During the lesson, if the early career teacher missed something, the mentor held up a mini whiteboard directing her attention, enabling her to address this. When she was getting it right, he held up a whiteboard saying 'Brilliant', so she knew she was on the right track. This in-the-moment feedback, focusing on that granular target, enabled the early career teacher to make rapid progress. Her whole lesson was set on a different course and the pupils made far more progress.

Reflective task ◀◀◀

- When you are receiving feedback after an observation, can you always remember the specific moment your mentor is discussing?

- If, during independent practice, you observed a pupil making an error, would you wait until later to address it or would you give them in-the-moment feedback to redirect them?

If in-the-moment feedback works for your pupils, then discuss with your mentor whether they can give you in-the-moment feedback/coaching to redirect you. The two questions in this reflective task were highlighted to me during training with Chris Moyse. An excellent phrase he uses when discussing staff development is 'one size fits one', meaning every early career teacher will need support across different areas. I urge you to watch his webinars and read his blogs as detailed in the further reading.

Reflective task ◀◀◀

Retrieval practice again.

- Why is the 'I do, we do, you do' methodology of teaching with modelling important?

- Name two methods you could use to check prior knowledge of pupils before beginning your teacher exposition.

- List four assessment/questioning strategies you can use.

- Why is 'challenge with support' important? Which strategy was highlighted several times in the last chapter as a 'quick win'?

- Do you need to check who completes extension activities and how can you do this?

- What is the purpose of an 'exit ticket'?

So what?

Let's revisit those questions from the beginning of the chapter.

» *How do you balance your work and life and not get overloaded?* You achieve this by having a realistic desire to improve but by being granular about your next steps rather than trying to address everything every lesson. Using the planning methodology from Chapters 4 and 5 consistently will not only drive the progress of your pupils but be a framework that, with practice, embeds planning into your long-term memory. Cutting down your planning time and being smart about how you mark (eg live marking and whole-class feedback) will improve your work–life balance. Being reflective and really focusing your attention on marginal gains will give you good traction to move *furthest forward fastest.* And you need to know when to stop: there is no point staying up until 1am planning as your delivery will suffer. Ensure you use all of your department resources rather than trying to reinvent the wheel; just adapt them for your context.

» *How do you focus your attention on how to drive your development forward?* Use the statements from the frameworks to identify where you need to improve. Then use video recordings of yourself combined with live feedback from your mentor to drill down your strengths, weaknesses and next steps. Ensure you have clarity about what a 10 out of 10 looks like and the small steps to achieve progress from where you are now increased by +1 or +0.1.

» *When does it all get easier?* It really does get easier to plan lessons. Using the framework from Chapters 4 and 5 should already have made this process quicker for you. Prioritise and be organised. And always keep in mind you are doing this because you are changing lives. Use as many department resources as you can; do not reinvent the wheel. If someone has already found a great video, do not search YouTube for hours. Just work out how you can fit the resources to the 'I do, we do, you do' approach and contextualise to your own pupils.

Top tip ◀◀◀

Writing PowerPoint presentations takes a long time; it can be just as effective to communicate your precise learning points by writing them as you sit facing the class with your visualiser and lesson plan next to you as your reminder.

Now what? ◀ ◀ ◀

Practical ways to implement this in your classroom: tomorrow, next week, next year

Practical task for tomorrow ◀◀◀

- You are on a journey to becoming unconsciously competent. Answer the following questions and have a self-conversation about your next steps so that you are ready to GROW.

  - **G** – What is your *goal* in terms of maintaining a work–life balance yet constantly improving? How would it feel to have made real progress towards some of those 'learn that' and 'learn how to' teaching statements? What would it be like to achieve mastery of an area, yet not be overwhelmed with the time taken to get there?

  - **R** – What is your *reality* now? Are you struggling to manage time? Does it take you more time to plan than deliver your lessons? Do you have real clarity about what your next steps should be to get better?

  - **O** – What are your *options*? Look back at the top tips and your notes to help you reflect on practical strategies on how to get granular and rapidly improve you along that teaching continuum. Which ones could you do?

  - **W** – Commit. Which ones *will* you do? Can you think of any others? Write down a statement that says: 'I am going to focus on _____ by _____'.

- Look at your 'I will' list and choose one you can implement quickly. Commit to completing this tomorrow.

Practical task for next week ◀◀◀

Stop putting it off; speak to your designated safeguarding lead about recording yourself teach. Watch it back and, while being kind to yourself, identify something in your practice that you can improve. Work with you mentor with modelling, practice and live feedback to really make progress towards that target.

Practical task for the long term ◀◀◀

Write a date six weeks from now in your diary. When you get to that date, reflect on your progress (could you record yourself again and compare to the original?). Think about how long it is now taking you to plan lessons and, if it has not decreased, look back at the previous chapter for guidance.

Reflective task ◀◀◀

- Do you have a new-found or deeper understanding of how to make deliberate progress and how to use techniques from this book to support your work–life balance? Mark your scale bar again. Hopefully it is further on than at the start of the chapter.

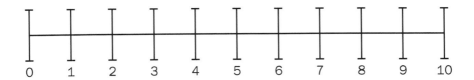

What next? ◀ ◀ ◀

You're nearly there. You have a structure to use every time you plan a lesson. You know the importance of human-first teaching and establishing simple rules and routines. Everything we have done until this point is based on research, notably around Rosenshine's principles. You have seen retrieval practice and introducing material modelled through the structure of this book and I hope you can see the benefits of these approaches and apply them to the pupils you teach. The last chapter will signpost some extra resources and give you some more top tips so that you really are ready to get out there and change lives.

Further reading

Books and websites that had a huge impact on my teaching

Ginnis, P (2005) *The Teacher's Toolkit*. Norwalk, CT: Crown House.

Griffith, A and Burns, M (2014) *Teaching Backward*. Norwalk, CT: Crown House.

Hattie, J (2012) *Visible Learning for Teachers*. London: Routledge.

Moyse, C (2021) Chris Moyse – TLC Education Services Limited. [online] Available at: https://chrismoyse.wordpress.com (accessed 6 September 2021).

The Learning Scientists has lots of downloadable resources, dual-coded printouts you can stick in your teacher's planner as reminders: The Learning Scientists (2021) [online] Available at: www.learningscientists.org (accessed 6 September 2021).

Chapter 7   Get out there and change lives!

What? (The big idea)

Last-minute tips, resources and reflections

>> What should you do if you have a bad day despite how hard you have worked?

>> Are you ready to get out there and be a human-first teacher armed with cognitive science informed frameworks?

This book has provided a deep understanding of how to get pupils to respond to you positively and then a framework on which to plan your lessons with a go-to methodology that ensures good outcomes for your pupils. This chapter includes some final top tips, extra ideas for resources and advice for when it is not going as smoothly as it might do.

Reflective task ◀◀◀

- In pencil, mark on the scale bar your readiness to be a positive force for your pupils. Consider all the things teachers worry about: behaviour, planning, managing workload, to name just a few. The higher the number on the scale, the more positive you feel.

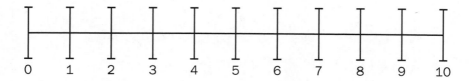

So, what if you have a really bad day or week and start to lose confidence in yourself? This is something that needs to be talked about. You'll have put your heart and soul into the job and worked really hard but sometimes it just all goes wrong. Either you get feedback that was difficult to take, have numerous deadlines to meet that feels like you are spinning plates, or maybe the behaviour of a pupil just gets under your skin.

Reflective task ◀◀◀

- What can you do when you feel like this? Who can you talk to?

- What practices from the book can you recall that will help?

You are human and the job of teaching is hugely demanding. Yet unlike some other professions, there is a real opportunity to build yourself back up again because of the rewarding nature of the job.

» The first step is to accept that this is going to happen and know when to seek support from your mentor. If you are really struggling, they can also signpost professional support.

» You can also talk to friends and family, even if it is just to unload.

» Think what you would say if someone was in the same situation; say those words to yourself and, more importantly, believe them.

» Remember those top tips from Chapter 2. When a pupil/parent/colleague gives you positive feedback, put it in a box or scrapbook. Re-reading these messages will remind you just what a difference you are making. When you have to make difficult phone calls or write sensitive emails, ensure you send twice the number of positive to negative ones. Parents are overwhelmingly grateful for positive feedback about their children and it is really exhilarating to feel this reflected back.

» Practise gratefulness (writing five things every day that you are grateful for) and mindfulness (even if it is just slow deliberate breathing).

» Another task to revisit from Chapter 2 is your 'why'. Think back to why you trained to be a teacher because the essence of that won't have changed: most likely, you wanted to make a positive difference and my goodness you will be!

» Remember that all behaviour is communication. Sometimes it feels really hard and despite all advice, you take things personally when a pupil just won't respond to you. Consider that what is going on in their lives could be so huge that you just can't have the immediate impact you desire. Two things to hold on to: even if in that moment you feel like you are not helping, that pupil will definitely remember you as 'the teacher that cared'; and secondly, there are probably 29 other pupils going home that you have helped. We tend to focus on the one child who is displaying difficult behaviours but forget about all the others who did exactly as we asked and produced lovely work. Focus your feelings on those pupils instead, or as well.

» And finally, use the GROW model. Sit and write out Goal, Reality, Options, Will and take decisive small steps to making yourself feel more positive. Taking control over situations and being solution driven will really help you professionally but can also be used for your personal life. Own your future, accept some days will be harder than others and that this is the same for all humans everywhere, and be empowered. In time, you will build confidence with the GROW model and find yourself practising it with your pupils and others in your life.

Most of the time, you will love your job despite how much hard work it is. And hopefully you will want to keep getting better, even as you become much more confident.

Reflective task ◀◀◀

- What else do you need to do to feel ready and empowered to change lives? Perhaps flick back through the book and use sticky notes to highlight particularly helpful pages or ideas.

So what? ◀ ◀ ◀

You should now feel ready to get out there and be a human-first teacher armed with cognitive science informed frameworks.

Now what? ◀ ◀ ◀

Practical ways to implement this in your classroom: tomorrow, next week, next year

Practical task for tomorrow ◀ ◀ ◀

Choose three pupils who have just shone this week and spend ten minutes writing an email/postcard home. Being pro-actively positive makes you feel really good and reaffirms what an impact you are making.

Practical task for next week ◀ ◀ ◀

Reflect on a lesson or an incident that did not go so well last week and left you with negative feelings. Now you have had some space, what can you do differently next time? Is there an expert colleague you can seek advice from? Can you do something positive, like contact the parents of a pupil, to assuage how you feel? Being solution driven and committing to making those changes can break any negative cycles.

Practical task for the long term ◀ ◀ ◀

Think about how you can be 10 per cent braver in your new-found confidence. Some schools are in their infancy on the road to using cognitive science informed pedagogy so you will have some great CPD you could offer, either to your department or to the wider school. Do not think for a minute that just because you are an early career teacher that other teachers cannot learn from you; be caring and sharing with all of your new-found knowledge!

What next? ◀ ◀ ◀

This is it. You are fully fledged, equipped and I hope informed about how you can be an amazing teacher. Jaz Ampaw-Farr gives out badges which proudly proclaim: 'I'm a teacher, what is your superpower?' Believe that every single day; live and breathe it. You are a life-changer and are going to have a bigger impact on your pupils than you can ever possibly imagine. You will see pupils around town years after you finished teaching them and they will remember you and the impact you had. You will be talked about for a long, long time and your legacy will be that teacher who really cared. Good luck on your journey; get out there and change some lives!

Chapter 8   Conclusion

Just one more thing...

Below are some of my favourite teaching and learning ideas that really work and bring joy to me when I teach. They are there for when you just need a bit of inspiration, so dip back into the book every now and again to add a new one to your repertoire. All templates are available on the Google Drive linked to @DrKellyR on Twitter, and pictures of them in action are on my Twitter feed.

Fourteen excellent things you can do with sticky notes

1. **'I wish my teacher knew that**...' from Chapter 2.

2. **Exit tickets** as formative assessment as described in Chapter 5.

3. Tutor group activities such as playing '**Just a Minute**' from Radio 4. Get pupils to write a topic such as 'The day I found an alien in my bedroom'. Pupils have to talk for one minute on that topic but if they pause or repeat themselves, someone else gets to take over the topic until the minute is complete. Great activity for oracy in later primary.

4. Ask pupils to write **two truths and a lie** about themselves. Someone picks a sticky note and reads it out; the other pupils have to guess who wrote it and which one is the lie. Great activity for bonding and building relationships with a new group.

5. **Accountability statements:** give each pupil in your class(es) a sticky note at the beginning of the year and ask them to write down what they hope to achieve at the end of the year. This is a bit like the 'I will' statements from the GROW model of coaching. It could be 'to try not to call out'; 'to complete all of my homework on time'; 'to be kind every day'. For older pupils, this is a great activity to make them accountable for their own outcomes. Tell them to write down the grade *they* want to see at the end of the course. Not their parents, friends or teachers but the grade they themselves feel will make them proud. Then, underneath, what they are going to do to ensure they reach their self-set target? Displaying these in the room and referring to them is a powerful way to facilitate pupils taking ownership of their own outcomes. And it is a good team approach opportunity to show that you will support them to reach their personalised goals.

6. **Peer assessment:** give each pupil three sticky notes and then tell them they have to visit three other pupils' work and leave feedback which is Kind, Specific and Helpful. Using sticky notes can sometimes encourage reluctant writers to participate as they are a finite space.

7. **Revision tasks:** give pupils five blue sticky notes (worth 100 points), four greens (worth 200 points), three oranges (worth 300 points), two pinks (worth 400 points) and one yellow (worth 500 points). The colours are obviously just an example and it is not important which colour, just whichever you have most of! Ask the pupils to write questions in pairs using all the materials from the topic. The higher the number of points, the more difficult the questions should be. The next lesson, they visit each other's questions as a pair and compete to answer the most. The original pairs then mark the answers and points are awarded. This activity will reveal a lot about pupils' progress, their misconceptions and their confidence. It is also engaging as it is quite competitive, and is obviously differentiated due to the question difficulty. An easy win: effective lesson with good metacognitive skills.

8. **Differentiated questions:** use the Question Grid template from the Google Drive (see @DrKellyR on Twitter) and re-write questions in the boxes. Each pupil has a copy of the sheet, and you project an image of it onto the whiteboard. Pupils are given sticky notes and told to attempt as many questions as they can, one on each sticky note. As they complete questions, they come and stick it onto the corresponding box on your projected image. The traffic light buttons indicate the difficulty of the question. You can then live mark it and give instant feedback. The beauty of this is you can see which questions pupils are attempting, those that they are getting right or wrong and again any misconceptions. At the end of the lesson, the pupils can have all their sticky notes back and stick them in their books.

9. **Secret task:** if you see a pupil needs more challenge, write a secret task on a sticky note and put it on their desk. Alternatively, give two pupils who are flying a sticky note each and tell them to write a 'killer challenge question' for each other.

10. **Who am I?** Split your class into teams and one pupil from each team in turn has a sticky note on their head with a character/object they have to guess with the fewest 'yes/no' questions.

11. **Brainstorm tree:** give pupils sticky notes to brainstorm ideas around a task or topic. Collect them at the front and arrange them into groups as a basis for discussion.

12. For very young pupils, sticky notes can be used to '**vote**', eg 'put a pink sticky note on your favourite insect model'. Pupils can then talk about why they like it and this can be used for formative feedback.

13. **Viewpoint line**: pose a question and ask pupils to put their named sticky note on a continuum line. At various points you can ask them if they want to move their sticky note and why.

14. **Help board:** pupils can put a named sticky note on a 'help me board' when they get stuck. You can add variations like help time 1, 2 and 3 to limit the number of times they can ask for help and encourage independence. Another variation is allowing another pupil to offer the help apart from yourself.

More review tasks

1. **Challenge board:** split the class in two and arm them with board pens. They line up in their teams in front of the whiteboard and write one fact each about the topic before passing the pen to the next team member in a relay. You could do it for a duration of a song or against the timer and see which team wins. This is a pacey, competitive task that really engages pupils with revision.

2. **Dominoes:** give each pair a piece of A4 coloured card which has been photocopied so it is divided into 16 sections. These sections will be domino pieces. On the right-hand side of each domino piece, the pair write a question. On the left-hand side, they write the answer to the first one and so on so that they make a line. The cards are shuffled and packs exchanged in a competitive game of sorting each other's dominoes. Again, a great way to engage pupils with revision.

3. **Matching pairs:** an alternative to dominoes that may be more suitable for younger pupils is matching pairs. Give them some small pieces of card and ask them in pairs to write a question on one card with the answer on another card. Do this as many times as they can to make a matching pair set that other pairs of pupils can match up.

4. **Battleships:** overwrite the example on the next page with your questions (or get the pupils to come up with the questions). Make two versions, and print enough copies so that one half of the class has one set of questions and the other half has the other set. Then enjoy watching them play! Original template by @worcesterjonny.

BATTLESHIPS

Fleet:
- Aircraft Carrier
- Battleship
- Cruiser
- Cruiser
- Destroyer
- Destroyer
- Sub
- Sub
- Sub

	1	2	3	4	5	6	7	8	9	10
A	List five ionic bonding facts.	What is a weak intermolecular force?	Describe metallic bonding.	Draw the polymer unit of chloroethene.	Draw ethandioic acid.	Explain frac distillation.	Equation for combustion of octane?	Composition of today's atmosphere?	What created early atmosphere?	What happened as the Earth cooled?
B	What is a precipitate?	what is the ozone layer and how did it allow certain animals to evolve?	Name three greenhouse gases.	Describe a neutron.	*Cruiser*	*Cruiser*	*Cruiser*	What is Avogadro's number?	Formula of aluminium hydroxide?	What is a mole?
C	*Sub*	How to make ammonium chloride?	Draw dot cross for N_2.	Draw dot cross for methane.	What are the main effects of climate change?	Test for sulphate ions?	Draw a chloride ion.	What is mass of a Li atom?	Draw an oxygen molecule.	*Aircraft Carrier*
D	Draw a fractionating column.	How do catalysts work?	Properties of graphite.	Properties of metals linked to structure?	Properties of covalent compounds.	Equation for Group 1 metal with water?	Formula of iron (III) oxide?	Sketch cracking.	Why is cracking used?	*Aircraft Carrier*
E	Problems with disposing of polymers?	Drawbacks of nanoparticles?	Equation for combustion of ethanol.	*Cruiser*	*Cruiser*	What are three natural polymers?	Two ways ethanol can be produced?	Draw a sulfide ion.	How does Strong E. force lead to properties?	Draw energy profiles for endo and exo reactions.
F	Properties of ceramics?	*Destroyer*	Draw poly unit for ethandial and ethandioic acid.	Equation for fermentation of alcohol?	Advantages of recycling polymers?	Which sulfates are insoluble?	What is ionic bonding?	Name three uses of nanoparticles.	Why do metals conduct electricity?	What key words are needed for distillation?
G	Uses of graphite?	*Destroyer*	How do you carry out a flame test?	What does malleable mean?	Write out the solubility rules.	How many molecules in 12g of SO_2?	*Sub*	Which carbonates are soluble?	Draw methyl propanoate.	
H	What is special about Group 8?		Molar concentration of 112g dm-3 NaOH?	*Sub*	Which chlorides are insoluble?	How much does 5 moles of $CaCO_3$ weight?	Does Dr Riches like chocolate?	What is neutralisation?	Emp form of 3g Li, 24g C and 144g O?	Describe the greenhouse effect.
I	*Destroyer*	Draw bromine water test for ethene.	Draw polymer unit for polypropene.	Draw a magnesium ion.	Describe the structure of diamond (4 points).		How much $MgCl_2$ is made from 27g of Mg mixed with HCl?	Draw a molecule of sulfur.	Describe the greenhouse effect.	
J	*Destroyer*	Ionic equation for $CaCO_3$ with HCl.	Will you be mine?	What vol is 5 moles CO_2?	Draw an ester link.	Describe an experiment for halogen reactivity.	*Battleship*	*Battleship*	*Battleship*	*Battleship*

5. An alternative to the Battleships would be a **Tic Tac Toe** three by three grid, which may be more suitable for younger pupils. Pupils write questions on each square of the grid, which other pupils attempt to answer. Or you write questions on a grid that they have to answer in pairs.

6. **Gallery event:** if pupils have been working on a piece of art, a model, a piece of writing or a presentation, plan a 'gallery event'. This is where all the work is displayed in the class for appraisal. Invite a member of the senior leadership or another member of staff to visit the 'exhibition'. Pupils absolutely love the recognition and will put in that extra bit of effort, particularly if in advance they know a 'special guest' is coming to view their work. Take pictures of the work and share with all staff/parents if you have time.

Reflective task ◀◀◀

- How could these strategies be used with any of your groups? Can you see how they align with retrieval practice as a summary exercise?

- Can you think of others? (Please share your ideas with me via Twitter for me to pass on.)

Have fun trying, refining and creating your own resources. Ensure you share them with me so I can share them for others to try!

Acronym buster

Acronym	What does it stand for?	Notes/links
AfL	Assessment for learning	Or assessment of learning
B4L	Behaviour for learning	
CLT	Cognitive load theory	
EAL	English as an additional language	For children whose first home language is not English
ECF	Early career framework	
ECT	Early career teachers	
DfE	Department for Education	
GROW	Goal, Reality, Option, Will	Coaching technique
ITT	Initial teacher training	
MWB	Mini whiteboards	For assessment of learning
NASBTT	National Association for School-Based Teacher Training	
PLP	Precise learning points	To replace learning objectives!
RP	Retrieval practice	
SEND	Special educational needs and disabilities	
SENDCo	Special educational needs and disabilities coordinator	

Index

ABC questioning, 60, 64
  benefits, 64
  limitations, 65
assessment, 57
  ABC questioning, 64–5
  choral response, 65–6
  cold calling technique, 62–4
  and exit tickets, 71–2
  and feedback, 57, 66–71
  GROW model, 79
  knowing your pupils, 73–6
  and marking, 67–8
  mini whiteboards technique, 60–2
  peer assessment, 69
  practical tasks, 79–80
  pre-assessment, 58–9
  purposeful, 68–9
  techniques, 60

back-pocket challenge, 78
Battleships review task, 101
behaviour. *See also* expectations/high
    expectations
  as communication, 33–4, 95
  management of, 30, 31, 35–6
  modelling of, 20, 75
  school behaviour policies, 33, 39, 52
  teaching of, 36
Bennett, Tom, 30
brainstorm tree, 100
building schema, 7

challenge board review task, 101
choral response, 60, 65
  benefits, 66
  limitations, 66
cognitive load theory, 2, 9, 14, 76
  impact of, 5, 17
  importance of, 2
  in planning lessons, 42–3
cold calling, 60, 62–3
  benefits, 63
  limitations, 63
communication, behaviour as, 33–4, 95
competency building, 30, 84
  and development, 89

planning, 89
practical tasks, 90–1
and reflections, 84
work–life balance, 89
consistency, in behaviour management, 33
constructivist learning, 6
curriculum, 31, 43, 48

differentiated questions, 100
differentiation, 73, 76, 77
discovery, 6
Dix, Paul, 31
dominoes review task, 101
dual coding, 8, 9, 10, 13, 49, 50–1

educational gap, 8, 74
English as an additional language
    (EAL), 75
exit tickets, 71–2, 99
expectations/high expectations, 29–30, 35, 37,
    76, *See also* behaviour
  case studies, 35–6
  and human-first teacher, 35
  parental contact, 37
  practical tasks, 38–9
  pupils' behaviour, 30–1
  rigidity in, 35
  school behaviour policies, 33, 39, 52

feedback
  acceptance of, 85
  and assessment, 57
  during and after lessons, 66–71
  in-the-moment, 88
  peer feedback, 86–7
  positive feedback, 94

gallery event review task, 103
Ginott, Haim G, 27
glossaries, 76
gratefulness, 95
GROW model, 25–6, 95
  for assessment, 79
  for behaviour management, 38
  for competency building, 90
  for planning lessons, 53

help board, using sticky notes in, 101

high expectations. *See* expectations/high expectations

highlighting technique, 70

human-first teaching/teachers, 34, 74, 96
  becoming, 22
  and behaviour management, 35
  and behavioural teaching, 31
  case studies to understand, 23–4
  GROW coaching model, 25–6
  meaning of, 17–18, 24
  practical tasks, 13–14

instructions refusal, handling of, 36

interleaving, 6, 10, 44–5

Kirschner, Paul A, 6

learning capacity
  case studies, 23
  development of, 23

learning styles, 2

Lemov, Doug, 62

long-term memory, 3, 4–5, 7, 31

marking, 67–8

matching pairs review task, 101

memory, 7, 18

metacognition, 11–12, 13, 14, 18

mindfulness, 95

mini whiteboards, 60–1
  benefits, 61
  limitations, 61–2

moral duty, 20

new knowledge, learning of, 5–6

new learning, 47–8
  approaches, 51
  case studies, 48–9
  example, 49–50
  individual practices, 52
  introduce new material in small steps
    approach, 49, 50, 57, 77
  pupils working in silence, 52
  using dual coding in, 50–1

new skill, learning of, 5–6

one-voice rule, 32, 33, 36, 37, 39, 52

online timers, 52

organisation, 89

passion, 21

pastoral support, case study, 24

peer assessment, 69, 70–1, 100

peer feedback, 86–7

planning lessons, 76, 89
  based on cognitive science, 41–2
  case studies, 48–9
  case study, 43
  checking progress during or after a
    lesson, 71
  cognitive load theory, 42–3
  and differentiation, 73
  and exit tickets, 71–2
  'good' lessons, 42
  GROW model, 53
  introducing new material in small
    steps, 47–53
  practical tasks, 53–4
  retrieval practice, 43–7

positive communication, 37

practice, 7–8, 9

pre-assessment. *See* assessment

prioritisation, 89

professional development, 89

pupil premium pupils, 74

redundancy effect, 9

retrieval practice, 6, 10, 13, 18, 31, 44, 88–9
  dos and don'ts of, 45
  elements of, 10
  impact of, 58
  importance of, 8
  in planning lessons, 43–7
  process of, 46–7
  templates, 46

revision tasks, using sticky notes in, 100

Rosenshine, B, 6, 47

school behaviour policies, 33, 36, 39, 52

seating plan, 36, 73, 75, 76

secret task, using sticky notes in, 100

self-assessment, 69–71

short-term memory. *See* working memory

silent activity, 52

spaced practice, 6, 10, 18, 44

special educational needs and disabilities
  (SEND), 75–6

sticky notes, activities using
  accountability statements, 99
  brainstorm tree, 100
  differentiated questions, 100
  exit tickets, 99
  help board, 101
  'I wish my teacher knew that ...', 99
  peer assessment, 100
  relationship building activity, 99
  revision tasks, 100
  secret task, 100
  tutor group activities, 99
  viewpoint line, 101
  voting, 101
  'who am I' activity, 100
support seeking, 94
support, challenge with, 76-8
Sweller, John, 3

teacher
  competency building. See competency
    building
  feedback acceptance, 85
  reason for becoming a, 95
  recording lessons, 86-8
  reflections, 84, 85
teaching
  case studies, 20-1, 87-8
  GROW coaching model, 25-6
  'I do' part, 51, 53, 59, 70
  misconception of, 23
  as passion, 21
  reasons for, 19-21
  'we do' part, 51, 52, 59, 70
  'you do' part, 52, 53, 69, 70, 71, 72, 77

teaching demands
  nature of, 94-5
  practical tasks, 96
teaching strategies, 4, 5, 13, See also
    assessment
  dual coding, 8, 9, 10, 13, 49, 50-1
  interleaving, 6, 10, 44-5
  lesson plan. See planning lessons
  metacognitive, 11-12, 13, 14, 18
  practical tasks, 13
  retrieval practice. See retrieval practice
  spaced practice, 6, 10, 18, 44
'Think Harder' task, 78
Tic Tac Toe review task, 103

VAK (visual, auditory and kinaesthetic) learning
    styles, 2
Venn diagram, in assessment, 70
viewpoint line, using sticky notes in, 101
voting, using sticky notes in, 101

well-worn path, 75, 76
'who am I?' activity, 100
whole class feedback, 67-8
Wiliam, Dylan, 2, 68
Willingham, Daniel T, 4, 8
working memory, 3
  extraneous load, 4
  germane load, 4
  intrinsic load, 3
  overloading of, 9
work-life balance, 89